JUST NUISANCE AB

Greetings, shipmate! This picture of Just Nuisance, taken on board the destroyer HMS Encounter *at Simon's Town, was buried in the ground or hidden elsewhere with other personal belongings of Able Seaman Ray Stubbs of Newbury, Berkshire, in Japanese POW camps in Sumatra after* Encounter *was sunk by enemy action in the Java Sea.*

JUST NUISANCE, AB
His Full Story

by Terence Sisson

To my sea-dog oppo
Able Seaman Just Nuisance RN
and my wife and family

Cartoon illustrations
by Tony Grogan

W. J. FLESCH & PARTNERS (PTY) LTD

First Edition June 1985
ISBN 0 949989 38 X
Reprinted February 1986
Reprinted November 1987
Reprinted October 1989
Second Edition January 1991
ISBN 0 949989 51 7
Reprinted June 1997
Reprinted January 1999
Reprinted February 2001
Reprinted April 2003

FLESCH PUBLICATIONS cc
P.O. Box 31353, Grassy Park 7888
Telephone (021) 705 4317
E-mail: sflesch@iafrica.com

Printed and bound by Paarl Print
Oosterland Street, Paarl, South Africa

Contents

Foreword

by Vice-Admiral
James Johnson
SSA SM DSC

One hot day in 1979 my wife and I were motoring through England when we stopped at a very shipshape-looking pub at Southend-on-Sea, in my case to absorb a pint of draught bitter. Mine host had "ex-Navy" written all over him, so I tentatively asked whether he had been in the Service.

"That's right, sir," he replied. "Boy Seaman to Chief Petty Officer — over 20 years in the Andrew".

I identified myself as a member of the cloth — and a South African to boot.

"Well, sir," he exclaimed with enthusiasm, "then you would have known Just Nuisance!"

Before I could reply he called the regulars to attention. "Listen, everyone", he said, "this gentleman comes from Simon's Town in South Africa and he knew Just Nuisance. How many times have I told you about that lovely dog?"

From the murmers of assent it was clear that Just Nuisance figured frequently as a topic for discussion.

"Many is the time, sir, that he escorted me and my mates back to the ship. Tell you what, ladies and gentlemen," he announced, "the next round is on the house."

With our glasses filled, he then called on us to drink a toast "to the memory of Just Nuisance, the sailors' dog".

We joined the regulars who good-humouredly settled down to listen to an oft-told tale.

In the circumstances I dared not admit that I had never had the privilege of meeting this famous Able Seaman, although as a former resident of Simon's Town I had heard a great deal about him. The thought went through my mind that there must be hundreds of ex-matelots throughout the British Isles who would have been delighted to join us in our tribute.

Greyfriars Bobby is world famous. To my mind Just Nuisance is deserving of equal fame. Certainly his story is unique.

Sadly the accents of Scouse, Yorkie, Geordie, Taffy, Jock and Shirer are no longer heard in the streets of Simon's Town. However they will long be remembered with affection by South Africans, but none so much as the erstwhile shipmate of their forebears, Able Seaman Just Nuisance.

I commend Terence Sisson for his enterprise in writing this splendid book, and trust that it will enjoy a wide circulation.

He has earned the gratitude of all of us, not the least Mine Host of Southend-on-Sea, and his contemporaries.

James Johnson

St James
Cape Province
May 1985

Introduction

This is the story of a dog. A canine that is unique in the annals of war. He was the only dog ever to be officially enlisted in the ranks of the Royal Navy in peace or war.

His name was Just Nuisance. After enlistment in the Royal Navy on August 25 1939, his official rank and name was Able Seaman Just Nuisance.

He was also the only member of the senior service – from admiral of the fleet down to the lowest rank of ordinary seaman – to be excused by Admiralty Orders the wearing of a cap at any time.

He was sent as a "sprog" (newly joined recruit) to serve at *HMS Afrikander I*, a shore base naval establishment at Simon's Town, 25 miles round the coast from Cape Town. He was born, with a brother later known as Bats, at the Cape Town suburb of Rondebosch. His sire was called Koning and his dam was Diana, both parents thoroughbred Great Danes of notable pedigree.

His master was a Mr M. Bosman, a breeder of Great Danes, who sold him to a Mr B. J. Chaney, of the Cape Town suburb of Mowbray, when he was about 11 months old. It was apparent that he was to be massive, both in height and breadth of chest, when he reached maturity at about 15 months old – even for a Great Dane.

What names were given these two canines as puppies by Bosman is not known but it is irrelevant because they would have been forgotten anyway – after naval ratings allocated them the names of Nuisance and Bats when they both started frequenting the precincts of ships and the shore base at Simon's Town. Bats, however, was finally accepted as a guard dog at the Royal Navy Hospital at Simon's Town, but was never officially enrolled in the Royal Navy.

Little is known about their first year of life until Benjamin Chaney bought Nuisance, and he was registered before this event by the SA Kennel Union with the pedigree title, Pride of Rondebosch. Soon after buying Nuisance in March 1939 (born on April 1, 1937) the Chaneys were appointed to take charge of the United Services Institute at Simon's Town. This institute catered for the welfare and comfort of servicemen and women stationed at the naval base or in Royal Navy ships docked in Simon's Town Harbour.

By far the largest majority of the patrons were naval ratings – and most of these were from seaman branches of the Royal Navy whose uniforms were of the type known as "square rig" – that is bell-bottomed trousers and tight jumpers, with the familiar blue collar forming a V at the chest and hanging over the shoulder blades in a rectangle, bordered by three white stripes. Officers, chief petty officers, petty officers, and certain branches of the Royal Navy ratings, wore what was referred to as "fore-and-aft rig" – buttoned jackets and narrow trousers with ironed creases at the front and back. Their caps, unlike those of square-rig ratings, had peaks at the front.

The ordinary naval rating was more boisterous and jovial, towards both humans and animals, than officers and NCO's of the senior service and it is undoubtedly due to this that Nuisance preferred their company. He was known throughout his life as a ratings' dog.

As the book describes, there were exceptions to this rule applied by Nuisance. The statement, made even today, by people of the Cape Peninsula that Nuisance was never seen in the company of anyone but the bell-bottomed sailor is a fallacy. Amend the word 'never' to 'seldom', and that would be correct.

Human females he ignored. Great Dane bitches he loved.

Besides being present most days at the Institute, begging tit-bits from his rating friends, Nuisance was allowed on board ships of the Royal Navy moored in the Dockyard, and this is how he came to be christened Nuisance. He would accompany ratings (without a ticket) on the train from Simon's Town to Cape Town and his vendetta with the South African Railways officials who put him off the trains is recorded, with the eventual outcome of this feud. It was this that led up to his being accepted as an able seaman in His Majesty's Royal Navy.

The SAR informed Chaney that, unless Nuisance refrained from travelling on trains without a ticket he would be put to sleep. As Nuisance was by now a legend among both naval personnel and citizens of the Cape, there was an angry protest by thousands of people. Finally the Admiralty intervened, enlisted him in the Royal Navy and provided him with a complimentary railway ticket.

It is also a fact that during his entire naval career he never bit a human being, though several times he came close to doing that. Nor would he attack other dogs, unless they threatened him. Indisputably, he did kill other dogs. On August 4 1942 he caused the death of the dog mascot aboard *HMS Shropshire* and in November 1943, he killed the mascot of *HMS Redoubt*. He was exonerated on the grounds that both dogs attacked him first.

I did not arrive in Cape Town till November 1942, a 19-year-old in the Fleet Air Arm stationed at Royal Naval Air Station Wingfield about six miles inland from Cape Town at Goodwood. I stayed there till February 1944, and Nuisance became a companion (intermittently, as he never stayed long at any one place). How I achieved this friendship is told in this book.

To write of Nuisance's life and the highlights of his career from his birth in 1937 to his death in April 1944, it was essential that I contact ex-Navy personnel who knew him personally before I came to South Africa. This was achieved by appealing to three British national newspapers, more than two years ago, to publish a request for any ex-Navy officers, NCO's or ratings who were stationed at Simon's Town to contact me at my home address. I received 31 replies, all from ex-naval men who had known Nuisance personally. Their present homes ranged from the north of Scotland, down through England's middle counties, Wales and to the south coast. I eliminated all but nine of these, as in 22 cases the writers had known Nuisance only for a matter of a few days or a couple of weeks. But I had great good fortune in that two of my contacts had been escorts to Nuisance between 1939–42 at *HMS Afrikander I* and its satellite base of Froggy Pond five miles from Simon's Town. Also, two other ex-Royal Navy members were present when events occurred which had a profound influence on Nuisance's life.

The first person I visited was ex-Petty Officer J. Carter, of Inverness, Scotland, who was the rating on the train when a ticket-collector tried to evict Nuisance's canine friend Ajax, and was lucky to escape retribution by the Great Dane. I recorded his conversation on tape, his closing words being: "I'm certain that if I hadn't stepped in there'd have been a vacancy for a ticket collector."

The next reminiscence I recorded was that of ex-Chief Petty Officer G. Clark, of Fareham, near Portsmouth, who was escort of Nuisance at *Afrikander* and Froggy Pond. He was in attendance on many occasions when Nuisance was appearing before senior authority for punishment relating to breaches of Naval Regulations. He still has a piece of claw which a surgeon commander clipped from Nuisance's ingrowing nail, causing a bad limp. He also remembers clearly much of the dialogue which took place at these interviews. Of course, after more than 40 years, the words used are not verbatim but are accurate in context, and as authentic as his memory can recall.

Then I visited and tape-recorded the interview I had with ex-Petty Officer H. E. Brown, of Bethnal Green, London. He also provided much information and the dialogue while he was escort to Nuisance at *Afrikander I*. My final recorded interview was with ex-Lieutenant A. L. Gordon (Writer Branch) RN, of Leeds, Yorkshire, who was in charge of proceedings when Nuisance's Service Documents were completed. He explained how many of the entries on the documents were arrived at, including how Nuisance was given the Christian name of Just.

Five other interviews with different ex-naval ratings only confirmed facts about Nuisance that I already knew. However, I was grateful for the time and assistance they gave me.

I met Benjamin Chaney in Cape Town at the time Nuisance was accompanying me and I spent a pleasant three hours in his company after hearing his account of how he was once the dog's owner. He related several comical events before the Royal Navy acquired their canine AB. I have mentioned all these five people so the reader understands how I came by such information and dialogue dating from before my first meeting with

Nuisance. From then on, of course, I am able to recount incidents and events from first-hand experience regarding this legendary seaman.

I hope the reader enjoys this book as much as I did in writing it, in tribute to a canine able seaman who will be remembered by many generations to come – especially by the people of South Africa, and the Cape Peninsula in particular.

Acknowledgements

In writing a book of this type, the author is to a great extent dependent on contributed material, and I wish to express my sincere thanks to all those people living in South Africa – well over 400 of them – who responded to my published appeals for information about and photographs of Just Nuisance, to add to my personal memories of him.

Space limitation makes it impossible for me to acknowledge all these contributions individually, but I should like to name the following persons who have been particularly helpful in the compilation of this book: Roger Williams, chief reporter of the *Cape Times*, in Cape Town, who has been of inestimable help in so many ways that it is no exaggeration to say that without his assistance this book could not have been completed; The editors of the *Cape Times*, the *Daily News*, Durban, and the *Sunday Times*, Johannesburg, for publishing my requests for information and photographs;

Rhys Meier, the "Chiel" colomnist of the *Daily Dispatch*, East London, for sending me letters and photographs from his readers;

Mrs E. Biggs, curator of the Simon's Town Museum;

Leslie M. Steyn, for the personal gift of his booklet *Just Nuisance* (revised copy, 1968);

D. A. Jordan of Pinelands, Geoff Dawson of Durban, Mrs Greta King of Johannesburg, Peter King of East London, Mrs A. McCallum of Pinetown, Natal, Mrs I. Williams and Mrs B. Nielsen of Durbanville, Cape, Mrs Lois Alexander of Bloemfontein, Mrs E. Boulle of Bedfordview, Transvaal, C. Smith of East London and Mrs N. Smith of Johannesburg.

I should also like to thank Benjamin Chaney, who at Simon's Town in 1943 recounted to me his anecdotes concerning Just Nuisance when he was a puppy, and the following former members of the Royal Navy with whom I have been in touch:

Ray S. Stubbs of Newbury, Berks, who made available a photograph of Nuisance on board the destroyer *HMS Encounter*, when she called at Simon's Town during the war;

Ex-Petty Officer J. Carter of Inverness, Scotland, (the rating who rescued the ticket-collector when he tried to evict Ajax, the bulldog, from a train and Nuisance defended his canine "oppo");

Ex-Chief Petty Officer G. Clark of Fareham, Hants, who was escort to Nuisance at Froggy Pond and *HMS Afrikander I*;

Ex-Petty Officer H. E. Brown of Bethnal Green, London, who was escort to Nuisance at *HMS Afrikander I*; and ex-Lieutenant A. L. Gordon of Leeds, Yorkshire.

Just Nuisance in the company he loved — that of jolly jack tars. The picture was taken on board HMS Prince of Wales, *when the battleship called at Simon's Town in 1941. The* Prince of Wales *and the battle-cruiser* Repulse *were later sunk by Japanese torpedo bombers near Singapore.*

Young Nuisance

The dog who was to be the only officially-enlisted animal in the Royal Navy in peace or war, was born on April 1 1937. This April Fools' Day birth was definitely not an augury for the wisdom and intelligence he acquired as the dog grew to maturity.

He was born to a Great Dane bitch named Diana, while his sire was called Koning. Both his parents had high falutin' pedigrees. This naval dog was registered with the SA Kennel Union as The Pride of Rondebosch. The litter arrived in this world at the home of Mr M. Bosman, a breeder of Great Danes in the Cape Town suburb of Rondebosch. In spite of much research I have not been able to establish exactly how many puppies were born in this litter, but there were at least two, both male — one the naval canine later to be named Nuisance, and his brother eventually called Bats.

Bats was a naval slang term applied to any person who had abnormally long ears or large feet. What names were first given to them by Mr Bosman are not known and, for the purpose of this book, are irrelevant, as they would quickly have been forgotten anyway. But both Nuisance and Bats had their names conferred on them by men of the Royal Navy when they were about a year old, at the Naval Base at Simon's Town.

Little is known about the early months of their lives. However, it was evident that Nuisance, on reaching maturity when 15 months of age, was going to be massive. He was already much taller and broader than Bats, whose proportions were more consistent with a dog of his breed and age.

About this time Nuisance injured his tail, right at the tip, which refused to heal in spite of all remedies tried by his owner. This was logical as Nuisance was very friendly and would follow his master all round the house, his injured tail wagging with metronomic regularity to show his canine pleasure.

Inevitably the wound on the extremity of his appendage was constantly in contact with protruding objects inside every room, including the walls, furniture, and other household fittings, leaving streaks of blood everywhere.

A couple of weeks later, with Nuisance's sensitive extremity still unhealed, Bosman was reading his daily newspaper, when he noticed an advertisement asking any reader with a dog for sale to contact Benjamin Chaney, in the Cape Town suburb of Mowbray.

Bosman visited Benjamin, taking Nuisance along with him. Chaney had recently lost his own dog, a bull mastiff, and wished to buy another pet. Though a little startled when he first saw the Great Dane's huge size, he immediately took a liking to him and bought Nuisance from Bosman. The price he paid for the dog is not recorded.

Before he left Bosman explained to the dog's new owner about the sore on Nuisance's tail, suggesting that the dog should visit a vet for expert treatment.

That same afternoon Chaney with his huge new pet on a leash — the one he'd used for the bull mastiff — set off for Cape Town.

On arrival the animal doctor examined the tail and said, "It's obvious why this wound won't heal. There's no infection but the way this animal wags his tail suggests he's continually rattling this sore against all kinds of objects, with no chance for scar tissue to form. I'll smear it with an antiseptic cream, and bind it with adhesive tape. Leave the tape on for five days, then remove it. By that time I'm sure it will have healed.

"By the way, I should buy a very strong collar and chain leash — your hound is the most magnificent physical specimen of a dog I've ever had in my surgery. He's got the heart and lungs of a horse.

"I wouldn't mind owning him myself . . ."

The vet treated the wound, Chaney paid the fee, then went to a pet shop to buy the heftiest collar in their stock. This collar was of leather, more than 6 mm thick, 50 mm wide, and had two leather fastening straps which fitted into strong steel buckles. There were conical brass studs adorning the surface and a tough steel ring rivetted to the collar to which a name-tag could be fitted and which could also serve as an anchor point for a leash spring-clip. Chaney also bought a leash made of stainless steel links, 2 m long, with a leather loop at one end for a handhold. The shopkeeper had a set of brass discs in stock and, with steel letter dies, punched the name and address on the disc and clipped it to the collar's steel ring.

The new owner omitted to have the dog's own name added, as at that time he had not decided what the moniker was going to be.

This was fortunate, as the Great Dane was to be dubbed by the name which was to be his till he died by the ratings of the Royal Navy serving at Simon's Town. This happened a few months afterwards, and how and why he came by his name is explained later. There is no record of the name chosen by Benjamin Chaney for his pet before the date when the Admiralty admitted him to the ranks of the Royal Navy.

Nuisance's master returned home to Mowbray and led the mighty pooch all round the house so his pet could familiarise itself with the rooms, then took him out to the small back garden where a few shrubs grew.

Once back inside the house Chaney decided he would make himself a meat sandwich. So, with Nuisance at his heels, he walked into the kitchen, where a large refrigerator stood in a corner. He pressed the lever down, opened the fridge door, extracted a couple of slices of bread and a dish on which was a haunch of roasted mutton, sliced a piece from it, and made his sandwich. Then noticing Nuisance, who was on his hind-quarters with forepaws dangling, in a begging attitude, he cut another piece of meat about the size of his fist and held it out to the dog's slavering jaws. Nuisance took the morsel, dainty-like, gulped once, and the lump of meat disappeared down the throat as if it was no bigger than a peanut.

Next morning Chaney, with his wife, entered the kitchen and realised he had acquired a hound that had intelligence and ingenuity. The fridge door was wide open, the haunch of meat was missing from the platter inside, and Nuisance lay fast asleep near one wall with a mutton bone at his side picked clean as a whistle. Mrs Chaney laughed and remarked that the bone was as smooth as a tooth brush handle.

Nuisance, hearing someone in the room, lifted his head and opened huge jaws in a gaping yawn, rose slowly to his feet and promptly sat down again in his usual begging style, forepaws dangling and his floppy ears up-pointed as if he was listening to what was said, and obviously wanting a snack for breakfast.

Mrs Chaney reached in the fridge and took out a large tin of corned beef, opened it and said to her husband: "I'll give him all this meat and that should last him till suppertime."

The thrifty wife was a long way out in her estimate. She emptied all the meat on the dish, and in less than two minutes it was gone, Nuisance's long tongue lapping up the last few morsels.

Mrs Chaney gasped in amazement and commented that her husband had better at least double his dog food allowance, but showed that she, too, was fond of the dog by rubbing his ears.

Nuisance, licking his jowls, wandered over to the sink and gazed at the dripping tap. Placing his forelegs on the side of the bowl he started to lick the drops of water running from the tap spout. Benjamin Chaney took the hint and filled a large saucepan with water and put it down on the floor. Nuisance's tongue began its one-way action and he quickly slurped every drop, then ambled over to the kitchen door, rose up on his hind legs and his paws scratched at the door-knob.

His master opened the door and watched as Nuisance bounded across the back garden. The dog stopped near a bush by the fence and started to paw up the ground. He performed his two early-morning bodily functions and then used his hindlegs to kick the soil he'd excavated over the contaminated spot.

He turned and trotted back to his master standing in the doorway, sat down and held out a paw to shake.

Chaney later that day described Nuisance's methods of hygiene to his wife who remarked that Bosman certainly knew how a dog should be house-trained, but for a dog to feel the need of a hand-shake after his toilet was something quite new.

After all this Chaney proudly announced to his friends that he had a pooch that was almost human in concept and intelligence.

A few weeks after buying Nuisance, Chaney was put in charge of the United Services' Institute in Simon's Town, whose premises provided comforts for all men of the Royal Navy, Army, and Royal Air Force. But the vast majority of its customers were sailors.

Nuisance, of course, was always with him on the premises, presumably as a guard dog, and it was here that he developed his life-long fondness for seamen.

It was soon apparent that he preferred the company of sailors who wore the famous "square rig" — that is, uniforms with bell-bottomed trousers, tight jumpers with a V-shaped front and a blue collar hanging over the back from the nape of the neck to below the shoulder blades. The collar was edged with those three narrow stripes that were supposed to represent Admiral Lord Nelson's three great victories over the French fleet.

Nuisance would tolerate officers, petty officers and various branches of ratings in the Royal Navy — such as cooks, writers, sick-bay men and others — who wore uniforms known as "fore-and-aft" rig: narrow trousers, button-up jackets, collar-and-tie, and peaked caps. However, the dog would always attach himself to a rating who wore square rig, though never at any time did he prefer the company of any particular rating. He spread his favour with strict impartiality.

He would stay with a rating for several hours then, with no warning, would leave him and tag along with any other sailor in square rig who happened to be passing by. Large numbers of seamen tried all kinds of tricks to adopt him; but Nuisance was his own master, as his legal owner would be the first to confirm. Every effort to convert him to a personal pet ended in failure.

If any rating tried to prevent Nuisance from going his own way by holding the dog's collar, his great jaws would open menacingly, showing the hefty incisor teeth, the flesh on each side of his snout would wrinkle, the great head would turn, and a deep rumble sound in the deeply-muscled chest.

These warning signs were invariably successful in making the matelot remove his hand from the collar. No one had seen or heard of Nuisance biting any human being — but there was a first time for everything, and the victim could well be a rating who had tormented the dog beyond its limit of endurance.

There are also accounts of Nuisance interrupting two or more sailors involved in a fight. The dog would launch his body between the contestants, rearing up on his hind legs, and pushing the men apart with his front paws or running between their legs and bowling them over. Once they were separated Nuisance would walk between them growling, indicating that if the fight was resumed he'd act as a peacemaker once more.

Sometimes he would even grip a sailor's arm or leg in his jaws, preventing the man from moving, but the jaws never tightened with enough force to pierce the flesh or cause other damage. Several of these incidents are described in later chapters.

Soon after taking up his position at the Institute, Chaney bought another dog, a bulldog he named Ajax.

Nuisance was now fully-grown, being one metre in height to the top of his head, just under two metres standing upright on his rear legs, and weighed 67kg of bone and muscle — and, in spite of his voracious appetite, there wasn't extra fat anywhere on his body.

Surprisingly, Nuisance accepted Ajax's presence in the Chaney home with astonishing good nature. Usually the sight of any other dog would be enough to set the Great Dane off in angry pursuit, but this affability could have been because Nuisance enjoyed the most comfortable settee in the house while Ajax had to be content with a rug on the floor for his sleeping quarters. The boss had also bought Nuisance a large enamel bowl for his three hefty portions of meat each day, while the bulldog had to be content with a saucerful.

Nuisance about this time had gradually shown his contempt for drinking water and Mrs Chaney, who had come to adore the mighty canine, provided him with a quart of fresh cream milk every day, while Ajax had to put up with Adam's wine (water). Clearly Nuisance saw himself as one of the family, in view of the preferential treatment he received; Ajax was to be considered only as a kind of temporary lodger.

Gradually, however, the two dogs became good friends and if Nuisance saw a larger dog bothering Ajax he would give voice with an ear-shattering howl of rage and race to the rescue. The sight of Nuisance tearing down on them put terror into the hearts of all other dogs, and they'd take off like greyhounds. When the knight errant arrived little Ajax would lick Nuisance's forelegs (which was as high as his tongue could reach) while the Great Dane's long, broad tongue would soothe both of the bulldog's ears.

There was one spot, though, where Nuisance would not allow Ajax to enter — and that was inside the Institute. If Ajax attempted entry Nuisance would lift up his big damp black nose to the sky and give a single loud bark of disapproval which would send the bulldog scampering away.

It was a fact of life to Nuisance — no other dogs were to make friends of sailors. That was his privilege, and intruders of the canine family risked their lives if they infringed on Nuisance's demesne.

Unfortunately Nuisance considered every other dog who tried to make friends with his 'oppos' (naval term for opposite number or close friend) as natural enemies and acted accordingly.

A few months after the Chaneys first acquired Ajax, some ratings from *HMS Neptune*, a cruiser moored at Simon's Town, enticed Nuisance aboard, and it was on this vessel that he began his naval career and achieved his name.

It came about this way.

He had developed a habit of sunning himself, lying full length, in one of the most-used gangways aboard *Neptune*. Exasperated members of the crew had to walk round his supine body when going about their duties and, although they were all fond of the dog, their language directed at him was certainly not suitable for the ears of females and young children, or any religious person.

The epithets all had one basic theme, with four letter words comprising most of the complaint.

"You so-and-so nuisance, why don't you. . . . off?"

This epithet was used so often by the seamen, and petty officers too, that it soon became his generally-accepted name. It stayed with him all his days.

HMS Milford, a sloop anchored alongside the dog's adopted ship, had a Daschund dog for their pet, who Nuisance tolerated with disdain, but if this animal tried to board *Neptune*, the Great Dane would send it yelping on its way.

Another sloop, *HMS Londonderry*, lying nearby, had a bulldog aboard, and whenever Nuisance saw it on the mooring ramp, would chase it round the Dockyard. There is no evidence that he ever caught it, but if he had, there was a strong possibility there would have been one traditional British dog listed as "missing, killed in action."

Although Nuisance was docile and good-humoured to all humans — especially naval ratings, unless cruelly provoked by them, and even in those cases he would not bite them — the massive animal could be dangerous.

One large Alsatian who attacked Nuisance lay dead a minute later. The police sergeant who made out a report added a final comment in his notebook that. "It looked as if this Alsatian dog had been mauled by a lion."

The chief petty officer steward aboard *HMS Neptune* took a particular fancy to Nuisance and, though dressed in fore-and-aft uniform for which Nuisance had little or no affinity, he allowed the CPO to take him into Cape Town by train, the chief steward always buying a rail ticket for the dog.

Actually Nuisance had a very good reason for accompanying him. The chief had been feeding Nuisance regularly every day for the past few weeks with huge portions of corned beef and lamb chops, and doggy savvy recognised that a source of highly-edible food and drink was not to be snubbed, but regarded with friendship whatever type of uniform he wore. (I used exactly the same method for cultivating Nuisance's respect for me when I first met him three years later.)

At the end of that month when the chief steward had to make out his victualling list for rations consumed by the ship's company during the preceding four weeks, he was faced with a dilemma. He should have had a dozen more large tins of corned beef and an extra two dozen lamb chops in his foodstocks than the number listed. The chief, with 22 loyal years of service in the Royal Navy, was a wily old hand, and thought back to the Navy of Nelson's day when his counterpart was called the purser. Some of these men had made small fortunes fiddling ships' supplies of food, so he followed tradition.

Alongside the entry which read number of tins of corned beef consumed, he wrote: "Twenty-one, plus 12 cans which, when opened, proved to have meat unfit for human consumption and thus disposed of for reasons of health." He used the same method of account for the discrepancy of lamb chops, knowing the ship's captain who inspected the book each

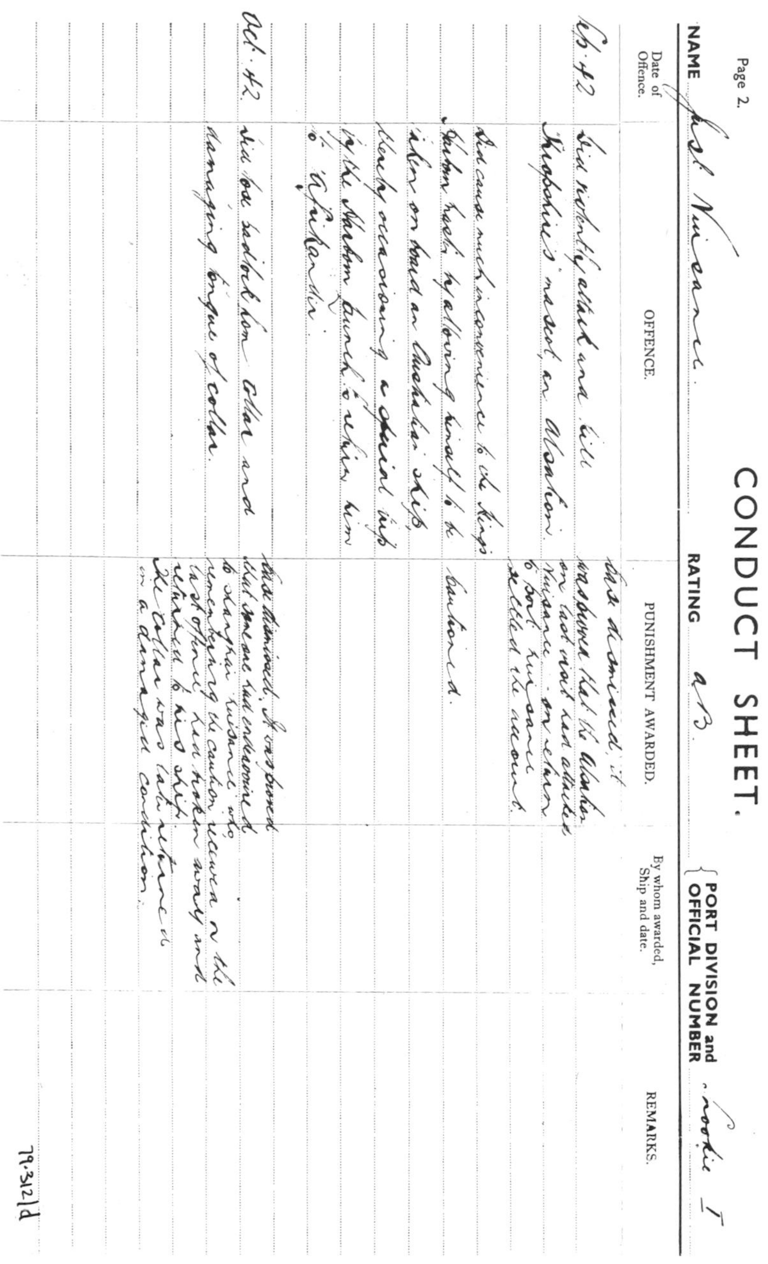

Page 2.

CONDUCT SHEET.

NAME Just Nuisance. RATING A.B. PORT DIVISION and OFFICIAL NUMBER Rookie I

Date of Offence.	OFFENCE.	PUNISHMENT AWARDED.	By whom awarded, Ship and date.	REMARKS.
Feb. 42	Did violently attack and kill "Shropshire's" mascot, an Alsatian.	Case dismissed, it was proved that the Alsatian on last visit had attacked Nuisance – on return to port Nuisance settled the account.		
	Did cause much inconvenience to the Kings Harbour Master by allowing himself to be taken on board an Australian ship, thereby occasioning a special trip by the Harbour Launch to return him to 'Afrikander'.	Cautioned.		
Oct. 42.	Did lose padlock from collar and damaging tongue of collar.	Case dismissed. It was proved that someone had endeavoured to shanghai Nuisance who remembering the caution received on the last offence, had broken away and returned to his ship. The collar was later returned in a damaged condition.		

79.312/d

The conduct sheet on which Nuisance's fatal attack on HMS Shropshire's *Alsatian mascot was recorded (See also page nine).*

month would accept the explanation of a senior NCO without question.

The repository, of course, for these items of food 'disposed of' was Nuisance's insatiable stomach.

The captain never queried the food returns but did comment to the chief that it was time the naval stores got rid of some food items which had probably been in their keeping for too many years. This was a stroke of good fortune for Nuisance, as he was not yet officially in the Royal Navy and therefore not entitled to rations; but the captain believed Nuisance was being fed from portions of food given to him by ratings.

Actually this assumption was partly true, Nuisance did accept pieces of meat from ratings in their mess-decks, in addition to the banquets he received from the chief steward.

Then it was that Nuisance started travelling by train from Simon's Town to Cape Town. He did this in the company of ratings who did not bother to buy him a ticket — thus starting a vendetta between Nuisance and officials of the South African Railways.

At first his oppos tried concealing him under the carriage seats, but his massive frame precluded this. The ticket-collector, with the help of the train guard, would eject the stowaway at the next station when the train halted. Often, before the train moved off again, Nuisance helped by his oppos would enter another carriage through an open door or window.

If he could not achieve this way of re-boarding the train before it moved off, Nuisance would walk down the track to the next station and wait patiently for the following train. Sometimes he would remain on the same railway platform on to which he'd been dumped, and simply catch the following train.

A few civvy passengers, especially women, would show apprehension when the Hercules of Dogdom boarded their compartments — but gradually they came to accept his presence, and even welcomed it. Eventually they even assisted the sailors' efforts to keep him on board and, quite often, they paid the ticket-collector for Nuisance's journeys to Cape Town.

Finally, however, Nuisance was being put off trains so frequently for not having a ticket that the South African Railways authorities informed Benjamin Chaney that unless the Great Dane was kept off their trains he would be destroyed.

The dog's proud owner simply could not guarantee that Nuisance would not board any more trains and, rather than see him immolated, decided to sell his pet. He would donate the proceeds to a popular cause called Speed the Planes Fund.

As these facts became known, ratings, petty officers and even commissioned officers raised a loud outcry in Simon's Town. Messages and memos flashed between various naval departments all round the Cape Peninsula. Even the naval C-in-C was involved. Then the Admiralty passed its official resolution. Nuisance was the mascot, and most-respected animal, of hundreds of sailors in both Simon's Town and Cape Town. Civilians in both these towns and suburbs also regarded him with enormous affection.

All were horrified at the news that Nuisance was to be sold to a private individual when it was obvious that the dog's place was with the men he regarded as oppos — the ratings of the Royal Navy.

The C-in-C South Atlantic was deluged by letters of protest about Nuisance and he then exercised his prerogative as Fleet Admiral and decreed that, although it set a precedent unequalled in naval history, the dog Nuisance was to be officially enlisted as a member of His Majesty King George VI's Royal Navy.

The Admiral issued orders to all senior naval officers in Simon's Town that Nuisance was to be accepted at once as a volunteer in the Senior Service.

Thus the steps were set in motion for Nuisance's enlistment as the first canine member of His Majesty's Forces, and he was on a rung of the ladder which was to lead him into many adventures.

Coincidentally, his brother Bats was also now involved with the Royal Navy, although never officially listed as a naval rating like Nuisance. However Bats was on the ration strength of the Royal Naval Hospital in Simon's Town, described as a 'guard dog.'

Why he was named Bats has never been clarified. This was naval slang for anyone who had abnormally large feet, but Nuisance, being much larger in all respects than his lesser-known brother, had much larger feet. Another explanation was possibly caused by some of the eccentricities Bats showed in his behaviour as a guard dog.

Bats' place of duty was the top of the concrete steps leading to the Hospital Block's offices. He would allow any person to pass up the steps and through the entrance; but he refused to let them down again. The naval rating who was in charge of the dog had to come out the door and hold him by the collar so that the individuals could leave. Perhaps Bats was rated as being in the bats-in-the-belfry category, but I suppose this alternative theory will never be resolved . . . .

It is a fact that on the few occasions that Nuisance and Bats confronted one another the result of a fight between the two brothers was a foregone conclusion. Nuisance was far larger, much heavier and stronger than Bats, but delighted sailors who watched the conflicts can vouch for the smaller Great Dane's courage in combat. No one tried to interfere as past contests between the brothers had proved that neither of them had suffered serious injury when, by mutual agreement, they both finished fighting.

Many onlookers also recounted that several times Nuisance had knocked Bats over and stood astride him — then let his opponent get up to resume the combat. They also found it strange that neither dog barked or growled when they battled — it was more like a wrestling contest between two friends who were only letting off energy and high spirits.

While Nuisance was waiting for his official 'calling up' papers to arrive, he initiated his oppo Ajax into the vagaries and tricks of obtaining free railway rides. Nuisance himself was now invulnerable to ticket-collectors, as they had been informed by their superiors that the British Admiralty had paid for a season ticket that allowed the dog to ride to Johannesburg if he so wished. He was not to be evicted from trains in the future.

The South African Railways officials would actually issue the pass in a few days and it would be attached to Nuisance's collar.

As Nuisance grew older he attained more wisdom. He sensed from the attitude of ticket-collectors, who now never came near him, that in some way he was a privileged being. His war with the railwaymen was a thing of the past. Whenever Nuisance boarded a train he would now sprawl across a seat, taking up enough space to accommodate three humans. Even when lying in a bed he would stretch out his great frame so that his head lay on the pillow; he never curled up like other dogs when they lay supine.

After all, this was the way his oppos slept, and so would he.

There had been many nights previously when Nuisance, having caught the last train from Cape Town to Simon's Town, could be seen stretched out on three seats covered with a sailor's greatcoat to keep out the chill night air while the owner of the coat would sit shivering near by.

Once, a bumptious ticket collector decided that even if Nuisance had permission to travel on trains without a ticket, he should be put in one of the dog-boxes of the rear carriage. With the assistance of two grinning sailors, who'd been asked to help, the ticket collector led them to the rear coach when the train stopped at Woodstock station. Nuisance followed

amiably, realising he wasn't being evicted; but when they got to the dog box they all saw that Nuisance's chest spread was 15cm more than the box's width.

Resignedly the ticket-collector led Nuisance back to his original seat accompanied by howls of mirth from his two naval assistants.

Nuisance barked once at the departing railway official to indicate his displeasure at having been disturbed (and the lack of respect accorded him) but the bark was so ear-shattering that other ratings in the same carriage swore that the official jumped high off the ground in fright. Other passengers in the coach placed their hands over their ears, and the windows of compartments near by were flung open and faces registering bewilderment or fright peered out.

One evening a few days later Nuisance, with Ajax the lodger trotting at his side, made his way to Simon's Town station. They stood together on the platform, Nuisance glowering at sailors who were patting Ajax's head after stroking his. When the train pulled in, Nuisance was the first passenger aboard (having two more legs than his naval oppos) then, standing in the doorway, saw that his small canine chum had a problem trying to get up into the carriage.

Ajax was less than 40cm high from the pads of his feet to the top of his head and, besides this, his legs were disproportionately short in comparison to his body. There was quite a gap between the platform edge, and the carriage foot-plate was 20cm higher than the concrete. Ajax struggled to board the coach several times, once nearly falling on the track.

Nuisance gave a wide yawn of disgust and jumped back on the platform.

He got behind Ajax, lowered his great head till it was beneath his chum's rump and catapulted the bulldog through the doorway with such force that the pug finished up not only in the carriage but curled up in a ball against the opposite side.

Nuisance re-boarded the train, placed one paw under his canine oppo's body and helped him regain his feet. Nuisance then trotted to a vacant spot, leapt up and spread across his usual space of three seats. Then he lowered his head and gently took hold of the loose skin on the top of Ajax's neck, and lifted the squat bulldog up to lie beside him.

When the ticket-collector arrived in the carriage he saw the two dogs lying on the seats near the window and turned to the nearest sailor and asked:

"I know the big dog man, it's Nuisance; he's allowed free rides but what about the other ugly beast, where's his ticket?"

The sailor smiled and jerked his thumb at Nuisance.

"Ask Nuisance mate, he brought him on the train."

The ticket-collector, looking at the sailor, added:

"Then the little dog will have to be put off at the next station, man."

"I wouldn't try it mister, unless you've a dozen strong men to help you — and even then I'd think twice about it . . ."

The ticket-collector ignored the warning and, at the next halt, arrived in the compartment accompanied by another official, and gripped Ajax by the collar to heave the bulldog out. The Great Dane's snout wrinkled with menace, the lion-like mouth gaped open showing two gleaming rows of upper and lower teeth. A low rumbling growl came from Nuisance's throat and the docile brown eyes somehow seemed to alter colour so they had glints of red in them.

With a snarl Nuisance launched himself from the seat, rose up on his hind legs, placed one paw each side of the ticket-collector's shoulders — and the pugnacious black nose and terrifying fangs were only millimetres from the man's throat.

The other official bolted through the carriage door, while Nuisance's victim, from whose face every vestige of blood had drained, looked as if he was about to faint. He turned a pleading face to the sailor and managed to whisper:

"For God's sake, man, get this animal off me, I've a wife and three young children. He'll kill me."

Although British sailors when ashore, especially in home ports, tend to play it up, by and large there is no more compassionate a man in the world than Jack Tar.

The sailor responded to the plea immediately. He, too, thought that Nuisance was about to bite a human being for the first time. The rating, who was billeted in the next hut to the Great Dane and knew him well, realised the danger.

If the Great Dane attacked the man, for all the affection people had for the dog, the South African authorities would have no choice but to order the animal 'put down'.

The young sailor approached Nuisance carefully, and gently placed one hand on the dog's head, and spoke in a soothing voice: "Come on Nuisance, old son; he's learnt his lesson, let him go."

Nuisance's eyes blinked a few times, then the rumbling growl ceased, his jowls closed, and he lowered his front paws, dropped them to the floor and walked quietly back to this seat and stretched out beside Ajax.

The sailor propped up the railwayman who looked as if he was about to collapse, opened the carriage door and yelled for assistance. Three railway officials appeared and led their colleague away.

After that whenever Nuisance and Ajax travelled by train together no ticket-collectors bothered them — obviously word had got around about the incident. Both dogs now enjoyed complete immunity from railway officialdom.

There are several recorded instances of Nuisance and Ajax being seen on the beaches at Sea Point and Muizenberg, running along the sea shore and paddling at the edge of the incoming surf, like children at play. Sometimes they would stop and dig holes in the sandy beaches. One report states that Ajax, on one of these sea-side outings, trod on some kind of sea creature (perhaps a sea snail) and Nuisance herded the limping bulldog into the shallow surf and made him walk up and down in the sea water.

He kept this up for about an hour and the salt water must have had a therapeutic effect on the sting because when Ajax left the beach he was no longer lame at all.

Was it coincidence or Nuisance's inherent wisdom that made him take Ajax into the surf? No one will ever know, but practically every onlooker at the beach believed in the latter theory.

In early June 1939 Nuisance, escorted by a rating, was taken to an office block at *HMS Afrikander I,* the shore-base at Simon's Town. This was a naval training barracks and a drafting depot whose function was to transfer sailors stationed there either aboard ships or to other naval bases controlled by the Royal Navy throughout the world.

A naval lieutenant and several ratings of the Writer (Clerical) Branch Royal Navy were in the room and their duties included filling in the application forms of volunteers. As Nuisance was setting a precedent for being the first canine to be enlisted in the Royal Navy, the completion of this form posed many problems.

Several answers to the questions on the form were left blank, to be resolved at a later date, and then Nuisance was taken by his escort to the sick-bay for a medical examination.

A surgeon-commander of the Royal Navy was responsible for the physical check on the dog, which was carried out thoroughly.

Finally the commander signed a medical certificate, which stated that Nuisance had passed AI, and was fit for the sea and active duty in any branch of the Service. He handed the rating this form and ordered him to escort Nuisance back to the recruiting office commenting: "Give the recruiting officer this certificate with my compliments and inform him that, in my opinion, if all ratings were as fit as this animal, there would be no requirements for a doctor at this depot."

Nuisance was taken back to the office and the lieutenant-writer looked at the medical form, and smiled when the rating informed him of the surgeon-commander's comments.

The officer patted Nuisance on the head and said: "Off you go Nuisance, we'll send for you in a few weeks' time, and perhaps by then we will have sorted out some of the answers when the day arrives for filling in your official enlistment papers. Once that's done, you'll be a naval rating in the Royal Navy."

Nuisance was fed up with the whole business and trotted out bound for the United Services Institute, where Benjamin Chaney gave him a celebration meal of roast beef.

According to Nuisance's Official Enlistment Documents these verify his date of enlistment and beginning of his service in the Royal Navy as August 25, 1939.

On Sunday, September 3, 1939, Great Britain declared war on Germany, and almost immediately countries of the Commonwealth (including South Africa) followed the UK's example.

Able Seaman Nuisance

On August 25 1939, in company with the same rating who had been his escort in June, Nuisance entered the recruiting office of *HMS Afrikander I* for his enlistment documents to be finalised.

This document is not made of ordinary paper. It has a linen texture, a folded double sheet. A copy of this document is on the next page, but there are one or two points concerning some of the entries in it which require clarification.

First, the lieutenant-writer decided on his own authority that the branch of the Royal Navy in which Nuisance was to serve should be the Signal, Seaman & W/T Branch. (W/T, of course, meaning wireless/telegraphist.)

The first problem arose when it came to filling in the heading listed as Christian Name. The lieutenant turned to his petty officer and asked:

"No dog has a Christian name PO, what the hell should I put here?"

The PO was not able to help his superior and replied:

"That's quite a poser sir, but I suppose we'll have to put something . . ."

"Well I can't see any other way out than to leave it blank, PO, and give the name as just Nuisance."

The PO looked at the lieutenant with a broad smile on his face:

"That's it sir, his Christian name, write 'Just' in that column."

The lieutenant did so – and it was in this way Nuisance gained a Christian name.

Then came the section which left all the clerical staff completely at a loss.

This required the rank of the seaman to be determined. The lieutenant felt that this should be authorised by higher authority and hurried along the corridor to the CO's office.

Once inside he explained his predicament to the senior officer who thought for a minute or two and then answered:

"It wouldn't be fair to rate him as an ordinary seaman, the lowest rank in his branch. Nuisance has really been an unofficial rating for about 18 months now and, all things being equal, if he'd been human he would have received promotion to able seaman. Obviously there'd be no point in making him a leading seaman, and he hasn't the necessary length of service to be rated petty officer. Put his rank as able seaman, lieutenant."

As the lieutenant re-entered his own office the PO had come across another conundrum in the document, and asked:

Just Nuisance's service certificate, issued at HMS Afrikander I, *the Royal Navy's shore establishment at Simon's Town in World War II.*

S.—459 (Revised—August, 1939).

CERTIFICATE of the Service of

SURNAME (In Block Letters)	CHRISTIAN NAME OR NAMES
Nuisance	First (Alias - Pride of Rondebosch)

in the Royal Navy.

NOTE.—The corner of this certificate is to be cut off where indicated if the man is discharged with a "Bad" character or with disgrace, or if specially directed by the Admiralty. If the corner is cut off, the fact is to be noted in the Ledger.

Port Division _Snookie._

Official No. _One_

Date of Birth _1st. April 1957._

Where born { Town or Village _Rondebosch._
County _C.P._

Man's Signature on discharge to Pension

Nearest known Relative or Friend.
(To be noted in pencil.)

Relationship :

Name :

Address :

Trade or occupation on entry _Bonecrusher._

Religious Denomination _Scroungos._

Sire - Koning.
Dam - Diana.

All Engagements, including Non-C.S., to be noted in these Columns.

Swimming Qualifications.

Date of actually volunteering	Commencement of time	Period volunteered for		Date.	Qualification.	Signature.
1. G.June '39	13 Aug '39	Period of Ida	1. Sep '39	PPP SA G/	
2.		present	2.		
3.		emergency.	3.		
4.			4.		
5.			5.		
6.			6.		

Medals, Clasps, &c., L.S. and G.C. Gratuity. (see also Page 4).

Date received or forfeited	Nature of Decoration	Date received or forfeited	Nature of Decoration

Description of Person	Stature		Chest, In.	Colour of			Marks, Wounds, and Scars
	Feet	In.		Hair	Eyes	Complexion	
On Entry as a Boy	2	6	26"	Blondy Brown	Yellow		
On advancement to man's rating, or on entry under 28 years		11					
On re-engagement or re-entry for C.S or for Non-C.S. after attaining 28 years							
Further description if necessary							

CAUTION : This is an Official document. Any alteration made to it without proper authority, will render the offender liable to severe penalties.

N. 7863/38.

(1331) Wt. 46307/D8824. 200M. 3/43 P.I. 51-6312

S. 459.

"What should be written under the heading Port Division and Official Number, sir?"

The officer was again bewildered. No one knew at that time where Nuisance would be stationed or, as the first dog in the Royal Navy, what his official number should be. The lieutenant decided the number had to be 1, but Port Division was insoluble. Again, using his own discretion, he wrote under this heading, Snoekie I.

Religion was noted as Canine Divinity League.

In the section which listed Promotions, Charges and Punishments this was, of course, left blank. The rating had only just joined; he was a sprog. But this space was, in time, to contain several entries, all under the Charges and Punishments category.

After the document had been completed there were sighs of relief from all members of the recruiting office. Nuisance had set another precedent. The completion of his service papers had taken twice as long to finalise as that for any other recruit.

Then Nuisance was led forward and gave a huge yawn, as his right paw was pressed on an ink pad and then pressed firmly down on the document at a line that read Rating's Signature.

On the lieutenant's orders Nuisance was then taken by his escort to a small workshop set up near the dockyard where an engine room artificer stamped Nuisance's name, rank and official number on a circular fibre disc about 25 mm in diameter and a couple of millimetres thick. This was the Identity disc which all officers and ratings wore round their necks, suspended by a loop of string or small chain.

The artificer then took a piece of brass about the same thickness as the disc, and with his metal shears cut out a piece about 40 mm long by 25 mm. On this, too, he stamped Nuisance's name, rank and number, but added the legend, South African Railways, Free Pass. The brass plate was drilled with a small hole at one edge, like the disc, and the artificer removed Nuisance's collar, fixed it in a vice and sawed through the collar's ring. He then threaded the disc and brass plate on the ring, rigged up his oxy-acetylene equipment and brazed the gap in the circular metal till it was a solid ring once more. He removed the surplus brazing material with a smooth file and polished it with emery paper.

While all this was going on, Nuisance had been sitting on his haunches gazing round the small room, utterly bored, and continually yawning – though there is no doubt that, if he had known what had been attached to his collar, he would have displayed extreme canine joy.

An identity disc exactly the same as his oppos wore — and a plate that informed any railway official that he was privileged to ride on trains without a ticket.

The SAR had also arranged that in a few days Nuisance would receive an official season ticket of strong cardboard which would be tied to his collar. This would be renewed whenever necessary.

The artificer signalled to the rating that his work was completed and patted Nusiance's head. The Great Dane ducked away from the petty officer artificer's hand, and nuzzled his escort's fingers – just to show that his friendship was reserved for sailors who wore square rig, not the fore-and-aft outfit worn by the journeyman.

The escort returned to the admin block and once more entered the recruiting office where the lieutenant-writer examined the disc and plate Nusiance now had on his collar, picked up a phone and reported to his CO that all enlistment procedures regarding Nusiance had been completed.

The lieutenant then handed the escort a small chit and ordered him to take Nusiance to the base clothing store, where the dog was to be issued with a rating's hat, and a new cap tally was to be tied round the rim and fixed with the small regulation bow.

When they arrived at the clothing store the chief petty officer in charge picked out a new seaman's cap and tally band then, with a grin on his face, placed the cap on Nusiance's head. The dog's usually-floppy ears perked up, and the hat just fitted between them; but the canine recruit showed his displeasure by ducking his massive nob, causing the cap to roll off.

The CPO determined not be be defeated by this sprog and pulled out the linen chin-strap tucked in the lining of the cap. He tied the head-dress on Nusiance's head again and this time pulled the strap tight so that it was firmly anchored.

Nusiance swung his head from side to side in an effort to remove this headgear. But it remained firmly in place and, finally Nusiance gave up the attempt to dislodge it.

His escort returned him to Benjamin Chaney who had already been informed that Nusiance was to be at the main gates of *HMS Afrikander I* at eight the next morning, complete with cap, as he was being transferred to a small naval barracks called Froggy Pond, five miles from Simon's Town, by lorry with two other ratings who had also been drafted to that camp.

Chaney, this being his last day as owner, was particularly generous to the dog. He laid on a royal feast, a plate piled with a dozen thick slices of roast beef, followed by a pudding of "spotted dick", with thick cream custard poured over it and, finally, a quart of fresh milk.

After this repast even Nusiance's huge appetite was sated, and he trotted into the Institute. As if realising he was to be parted from Ajax, for the first time he allowed the bulldog to enter the building and sleep alongside him on the Great Dane's favourite settee.

Next morning, promptly, Mr Chaney stood with Nusiance, wearing his new cap, at the main gates of *HMS Afrikander I*. Near them were two ratings carrying kit-bags and hammocks, also waiting for the transport lorry.

On arrival at Froggy Pond Naval Base, after the tail-gate of the lorry had been lowered, Nusiance leapt out and stared about him at his new quarters.

The two ratings, and Nuisance, were led to a small building in which the senior officer of the small base presided. Inside, the CO was at his desk with a chief petty officer by his side.

He briefed the two ratings as to the duties they were to carry out at Froggy Pond and what billets they'd been allocated, then dismissed them. Nuisance had sat patiently while the CO spoke, but stood up when the ratings left, his tail wagging frantically, the long wide tongue protruding from his jaws. The CO turned to the CPO and gestured at a document that lay on his desk, saying:

"It seems that the CO of *Afrikander* has requested certain privileges for Able Seaman Nuisance which, of course, will be granted. Commander Shakespear has always been known for his sense of humour, and requests that this rating be assigned in charge of all dog-watches. Secondly, regarding his victualling, he is to feed at the same time as all ratings stationed here, but is to be allotted only milk for drink, and meat or bones as his food. No salads, vegetables, nor any fruit which he refused to eat. His place of eating will be in the cook-house of the dining hall and, once a day, at dinner-time preferably, is to be given a large helping of spotted dick, this apparently being the only sweet he likes.

"Able Seaman Nuisance will be billeted in Number One Hut with sheet, blankets, pillow and mattress provided for his bunk. He is to be given shore leave each night and allowed all-night leave. At week-ends he has permission to go ashore from noon Saturdays and Sundays, till 7.30 a.m. the following days.

"The senior rating in charge of Hut One is to report any breaches of discipline inside that billet by this new rating. Will you see to that, please, Chief?"

"Aye, aye sir," replied the CPO and accompanied Nuisance out of the office and took him to his billet, Hut Number One.

When they arrived there the hut – which had two rows of bunks opposite each other along the walls, leaving an open space down the middle – was empty except for a leading seaman who was in charge of all ratings billeted there. He sat on a wooden form at a long table placed in the middle of the corridor space.

As the CPO and Nuisance entered the sailor rose to his feet, a beaming smile on his face. This seaman was tall and very broad – in fact he was the heavyweight boxing champion of all the Peninsula's armed services.

The CPO walked forward and Nuisance followed, and the NCO said: "Leading Seaman Clark, Able Seaman Nuisance is to be berthed in this hut under your charge. He has no duties and may accompany any rating from this or any other hut round the base. He will take his meals in the cook-house at the same times that ratings eat in the dining hall. You will allocate him a bunk and see that it is made tidy each morning. He is allowed ashore every evening in mid-week, and all week-ends.

"If there are any complaints about him please report to me, and also see to the matter of his cap being worn at all times when outside this berth and the removal of it when he retires at night."

The big leading seaman patted Nuisance on the head and replied: "We heard rumours that Nuisance was coming here chief, but the lads here will be over the moon when they learn he's to be in this hut. Some of them have been in his company at Cape Town; so have I for that matter. There'll be no trouble with him."

The CPO waved his hand at the seaman and left.

The leading seaman turned to Nuisance, who was sitting in a begging position, front paws dangling, then said:

"Alright Nuisance, I can take a hint – had no breakfast, right? Come on then, let's go and see my oppo the PO cook to find out if he can feed you."

Nuisance trotted contentedly behind the seaman as if the dog understood he was being taken for a meal. When they reached the cook-house, or galley as most ratings call it, the seaman had a word with the cook who stroked the dog's head and spoke to the seaman.

"OK mate, we already have a memo pinned up in here about Nuisance and his rations, I'll slice up a can of corned beef and then give him a bowl of milk."

When the sliced beef was placed in front of him Nuisance, anxious to show he was no gannet, delicately pawed each slice off the plate before eating it. In two minutes the meat was gone and, one minute later, he had disposed of the milk. The cook had watched him with an expression of awe on his face and murmured:

"I've heard about his appetite but this is the first time I've seen or watched it – tell you something mate, I'd rather keep him for a week than a fortnight, any time."

The seaman laughed and took Nuisance back to the billet.

Two hours later several ratings entered the hut and whooped with delight when they saw Nuisance. One of them took a carton of chocolate biscuits out of one of the lockers at the side of each bunk, and the dog polished them off faster than the rating could get them out of the box. Then Nuisance made for the door and the leading seaman followed him, beckoning for the other ratings to follow. When he got to the door he pointed to the dog who had raced to a piece of clear ground about a 100 metres from any hut, and the seaman predicted: "Watch him mates, he's off to do his business. I've heard about this from a mate of mine at *Afrikander*, he reckons this dog is as clean in his habits as any navy stoker."

(It was a recognised fact throughout the Royal Navy that the Stoker Branch were the most fanatical for cleanliness in both body and clothing possibly because on board ship they had the dirtiest duties to perform, and compensated for this when off watch.)

The ratings stood outside the hut door and watched Nuisance perform his ablutions. He dug a hole in the ground with his forepaws, turned, squatted over the hole for a couple of minutes, stood up and scraped back the upturned pile of earth. Then he sat on his haunches and dragged himself over the ground for 50 metres or so, rose to his feet and loped back to the hut.

Once there he licked the pads of his front paws and then the two back-leg pads, barked a single ear-shattering roar and held out his front paw to be shaken. The leading seaman did so and, facing the ratings who stood behind him, remarked:

"That's Nuisance's habits mates, I bet he's got the cleanest backside and feet in this hut. No need to worry about his bed sheet being clean."

The others roared with laughter and one of them exclaimed, "He's a bloody marvel is Nuisance mates, but he's got a big advantage over us as well. No uniform to press with an iron, no collars or underclothes to want dhobying, nor boots or shoes to brush – the old bugger's got it made, hasn't he killick?"

The leading seaman grinned and replied,

"I'll tell you something else – Nuisance won't let anyone put him in a bath, and there's sense in that, lying in your own dirt after a bath, aren't we? Always wants a shower, with somebody to soap him all over, and then he stands under the water-rose till all the suds have gone. Mate of mine over at *Afrikander* told me about that, so Nuisance gets a good wash down every day in our shower hut and will enjoy every minute of it, my oppo reckons."

A few days later the leading seaman was detailed to go in a lorry to *Afrikander* to pick up stores and took Nuisance with him.

On arrival, Nuisance jumped from the vehicle and set off for the Institute. As he reached the steps there was a low gruff bark and Ajax came running down the steps. There was no doubt that Nuisance was pleased to see his ex-lodger. He placed one great paw on the bulldog's back, and then commenced to lick the pug-nosed face, after which they entered the building. Superintendant Chaney was also delighted with his old pet's unexpected visit, and hunted out some meaty bones. The canine able seaman showed his appreciation of this welcome by holding out his right paw for his ex-master to shake.

Ajax, sensing that Nuisance was glad they were together once more, joined the Great Dane in his feast. This was something he would not have dared to have attempted a few days ago; but this time Nuisance even gripped one of the bones in his teeth and dropped it in front of Ajax's nose, placing his foreleg against his canine oppo's body and urging him to accept the offering.

Ajax ducked his head, gave a sharp yelp of excitement, and stretched out alongside nis mighty guardian and commenced gnawing the bone.

After a while Nuisance realised it was time to leave, so he licked Ajax's ears, then the massive head lowered and he gently butted the bulldog towards the Institute's serving area, and made his way to the door.

As he left Nuisance turned for a brief moment, and saw Mr Chaney waving farewell, while Ajax was looking forlornly in his direction. So Nuisance lifted up his head and gave one lion-like roar of farewell that woke up three naval ratings and a soldier, who had been lying asleep on a settee and arm-chairs, then disappeared on his way back to *Afrikander* and his oppo the leading seaman.

After being stationed at Froggy Pond for two weeks, Nuisance had established a close rapport with the PO cook (even if he did wear fore-and-aft rig) and made two or three unauthorised visits each day to the galley where there was always a plateful of meaty tit-bits put down for his consumption. The cook always remarked to his staff that he didn't want to be acccused of causing the animal to suffer from malnutrition. Once he added a remark which within a couple of hours was known all round the camp, except in the officers' quarters. The cook declared to all his galley staff, and a couple of PO's who were off-duty enjoying a glass of beer with them:

"Now if all the ratings in this billet respected my cooking like that bloody Hound of the Baskervilles does, then they might get even better grub than they do now."

In his two-weeks' stay at Froggy Pond, Nuisance had become friendly with officers, petty officers, and ratings in the small base, but was gaining a reputation as a bit of a trouble-making skate. One of Nuisance's many offences was being caught having a kip in his bunk during the daytime when the rest of the ratings in his billet were engaged in official duties. Four times in less than a week enraged petty officers on their inspections of the huts had seen Nuisance fast asleep in his billet and had led him before the officer-of-the-day charged with being asleep during recognised duty hours.

In every case, when these officers checked the duty list in the admin block they found Able Seaman Nuisance's name on it, with the CO's signature, that he had no official watch and was excused all duties, except for having to parade with all personnel on the base when the CO so commanded.

Nuisance's kips had not coincided with any parades, so the PO's were themselves chided for wasting the officer-of-the-day's time. The petty officers then accepted that Nuisance could be in his bunk all day and night without infringing regulations and ignored these frequent kips.

The base's CO was heard to complain to his Number 1 (second-in-command) that when all personnel were on parade, including Nuisance with his sailor's cap tied securely between his ears, that the rating never wagged his tail in acknowledgement to a senior officer.

The CO on these inspection parades would walk down the files of men under his command, checking uniforms, caps and boots, also the length of their hair. If he considered it too long for naval standards, he would announce to the master-at-arms who accompanied him that the rating must get his hair trimmed immediately the parade was over.

Nuisance never had any problems over hair-cutting; his fawn coat was always short and was always brushed by one of his oppos in the hut just before appearing on parade.

If Nuisance happened to be present when the camp's white ensign was lowered from its pole each evening at sunset the dog, like other ratings who were nearby, would stand at attention, tail nearly vertical, and quite still. When the short ceremony was finished, he would trot off to his billet, tail wagging furiously, knowing he had done his duty in a seemly manner.

Then after his evening meal in the galley, he would make for the guard-house, and then to the railway station for his usual visit to Cape Town. Nuisance was the only rating who had no watch card, a small doubled piece of stout cardboard, on the inside of which was printed the rating's name, rank, official number, and watch division. (Red for port watch, or green for starboard watch). When all ratings below commissioned rank went ashore, these cards were handed in at the guardhouse and collected by their owners on return. This way a check was kept on whoever was adrift and he would be put on a charge.

Commissioned officers signed a book when they went ashore, and then re-entered their names on their return.

The master-at-arms (senior warrant officer of all the three branches of His Majesty's armed forces) decided that although Nuisance, on the CO's orders, had not been detailed for any watch, he should at least have a watch card made out. He would be logged in and out of the base like all other ratings. A card was duly made out for the canine AB, a small hole pierced in it through which was threaded a piece of strong cord, and this was then tied by one of the MAA's staff to the ring on Nuisance's collar.

Unfortunately the cord had been made too long and the dog was able to move the collar slightly till he managed to get his teeth into this dangling appendage which irritated him by swinging against his neck as he walked. When he arrived at the guardroom that evening to go ashore in the company of Leading Seaman Clark, one of the guards, an able seaman who had been warned that Nuisance now had a watch card, stepped out from behind the guardroom's wooden barrier to remove the card from the collar.

He stared in disbelief at the ragged pulp still attached to the cord; it resembled a large piece of chewing gum. He untied the cord and spoke to the big leading seaman.

"The MAA will have a fit when he sees this killick, we've had specific instructions that Nuisance has to have his watch card removed when he goes ashore. I'd better not let him leave the base till this has been sorted out."

Leading Seaman Clark laughed.

"Try to stop him mate, he'll knock you over like a nine-pin, the only way you'll keep him on base is to use that Webley revolver on your belt and if you try that, it will be over my dead body. Besides, you'd be shooting an able seaman of the Royal Navy, they'd bloody-well hang you from a ship's yardarm."

The guardroom AB allowed Nuisance to go ashore, but told the leading seaman he'd have to report the matter.

The next morning at nine Nuisance was summoned to the MAA's office, escorted by one of the regulating staff.

What transpired is not known, but the fact remains that Nuisance was never again issued with a liberty card. Whether it ever occurred to the MAA to tie the card up close to the ring is not known but he may have considered it, and discarded the idea, as when Nuisance retired to his bunk at night one of his oppos removed not only his cap but collar too, and Nuisance would have had ample opportunity to chew up a replacement card while the collar lay on top of the locker next to his bunk.

When Nuisance had been at Froggy Pond for about three months he had his first and only disagreement with a shipmate in the hut.

This rating, except for the big leading seaman, was the largest and strongest man in the hut. Though he was usually a quiet sort of chap, he could get very nasty if crossed by another rating, after he'd been on a thrash. On such occasions his oppos were careful either to ignore or avoid him.

As it happened, Nuisance had himself been ashore that night in Cape Town, and returned by the last train. He entered his billet half an hour after the large AB who'd had quite a skinful to drink and, being confused and tipsy, had climbed by mistake into Nuisance's bunk. He lay there snoring lustily.

Leading Seaman Clark had stayed in Cape Town for the night. If he had been present in the hut there is no doubt that the ugly incident which ensued would not have happened. Anyway Nuisance advanced to his bunk and nudged the man with his head, causing the dog's cap to fall off.

The sailor grunted and slept on. Nuisance then took hold of the bunk's blanket between his teeth and pulled it off the seaman. The drunken rating woke with a roar of anger and started lashing out with his fists. Another rating, whose bunk was near the switch, flicked on the electric lights as by now every rating in the hut was wide awake.

When the bunk's intruder saw Nuisance standing by his bed he broke into a torrent of four letter words,

"Bloody Nuisance, if you don't . . . off, I'll make . . . mincemeat out of you; find your own . . . berth, you stupid . . . four-legged . . . ."

He grabbed the blanket, pulled it over himself and lay down again.

Nuisance took it in his teeth and removed it once more. Shouting with rage, the sailor got up out of the bunk and advanced on the dog. The man's fists were clenched and flailing the air in front of Nuisance's black snout.

The Great Dane reared up on his hind legs, dodging a fist that lashed out at him, placed his forepaws on each side of the rating's shoulders and pushed him back with enough force to knock his adversary flat on his back. Then he stood astride him, with his gaping jaws and awesome teeth only centimetres from the man's throat. The whole room was silent, except for a low rumbling growl coming from the innards of the canine AB.

All the other ratings were sitting up in their bunks watching the scene with petrified apprehension.

The drunken man's face was drained of colour, and there was no doubt he thought his last moments were fast running out. Then four ratings gained enough courage to leap from their bunks and tackle Nuisance before his huge jaws closed on the victim's neck.

Whether Nuisance would have bitten the man is debatable but, like the incident of the ticket-collector on the train, if he had, the base's CO might have been writing a letter of condolence to the big rating's next of kin. Up to that time the dog had never been known to bite a human being – but, given enough provocation, any dog will even turn on its master. The problem with Nuisance was that he was of such immense size and had jaws so powerful that his bite could be lethal if he bit anyone in the throat.

The three ratings managed to calm Nuisance down, and coax him into his bunk, while the drunk was now completely sober and rose to his feet on legs that trembled so much they barely supported him. Finally aware that he had intruded into the dog's sanctum, he made his way to his own bunk.

As one rating unbuckled the collar from Nuisance's neck he spoke to the big sailor who, still looking pale, was preparing to lie down: "You bloody-well nearly had it that time Lofty; if Nuisance wasn't an oppo of all sailors there'd have been a naval funeral taking place in a couple of days."

Lofty got out of his bunk and carefully walked over to Nuisance's bunk, the dog watching him with its head lifted off the pillow and a low growl rumbling again.

Taking care not to get too near, Lofty knelt down and held out a tentative arm and spoke in a low voice:

"I'm sorry Nuisance; didn't know it was your bed; put it down to me being a stupid, drunken sodding matelot; shake hands mate and let's be oppos again. There's nobody thinks more of you than me, you know that chum; what about it, son? Forget it ever happened, eh?"

The growling ceased, but Nuisance stared Lofty right in the eyes for at least two minutes, never moving, then he yawned and held out his right paw, which Lofty shook with delight. Then he returned quickly to his bunk, climbed in and said to the rating by the light switch: "Alright oppo, put the lights out now, and thanks very much you three who got Nuisance off me. I won't forget you, I thought I was a goner for a second or two there. Good-night Nuisance."

There was the sound of the dog yawning once more, then a muted bark. He was returning Lofty's wishes for a nice long kip.

The next morning when Leading Seaman Clark returned to the billet he was informed of the incident and moved over to Lofty who was sitting on his bunk rubbing a throbbing head, thanks to the liquor he'd consumed the night before. The killick waved several other ratings away from Lofty's bed, indicating he wanted a quiet word in private with him. Then he stood over Lofty and, in a voice filled with anger, said:

"Lofty, I'm only going to say this once, so listen close. First, you're bloody lucky to be still alive, but bear one thing in mind, if Nuisance had killed you, the dog would have been put down, and though that wouldn't have helped you any, being dead, every rating in this camp – and I mean all of them – would have mourned him, which is more than can be said for you.

"There's two things in your favour which stop me from belting the daylights out of you this minute. One is that I know you like the dog as much as I do and, second, you rotten bastard, you had the guts to go and apologise to him. Now next time you get drunk stay in one of the services' clubs till the next morning, because if you ever come in pissed-up again to this billet, you have my solemn promise that I'll put you in hospital for a bloody month, besides wanting a set of false teeth from the dentist. Understood, Lofty?"

The two big seamen shook hands and, though the matter wasn't forgotten, nor ever would be, at least there was a permanent truce between Nuisance and his two big oppos.

There were several occasions in his future career when Nuisance did grip a person's arm or leg in his jaws with enough strength to prevent them moving away from him, but always without breaking skin, or crushing a bone – though doubtless the recipients of his attentions might have had a few bruises to remind them of the dog's potential power. But Nuisance would apply this pressure only for a few seconds, then allow his victim to retreat.

Nuisance had his own ideas as to what constituted crime and punishment.

He turned up late one night at the Union Jack Club in Cape Town, and found a sailor in the bed always reserved for him, the only naval rating to be granted this privilege.

After trying to roll this seaman out of his bed using one huge paw to turn him over, to his disgust he found the man was corpulent, not very tall but weighing about 16 stone.

Shaking his head in a resigned manner at a matelot who was still awake and knew Nuisance well, the dog trotted over to his oppo for the seaman to take off his hat, which he did, saying to Nuisance:

"He'll take some moving oppo, weighs more than two other sailors put together. Kip down on the floor, chum."

Nuisance stuck his big black moist nose in the air and looked as if he was about to raise his voice in protest, which would have woken up everybody in the club, but instead he walked to the bed where the intruder lay, took the blanket in his teeth, pulled it to one side and hopped into bed beside the fat sailor. He must have been sleeping off a thrash, or taken an overdose of sleeping tablets, because he never even moved . . . .

About an hour later there was a resounding thud as the fat sailor was pushed out of bed by Nuisance, who had probably decided that one rating in a bed was enough, but two ratings occupying one berth was not to be condoned. And it was Nuisance's bed, ergo there was only a simple problem to solve, who should lie on the floor?

The stout seaman grunted as he hit the deck, rolled over, and snored on. Nuisance gave a huge yawn and seconds later was asleep. The club manager had heard the bump and investigated. Seeing what had happened, he laughed and printed on a card the words, "Beware all who enter here; you do so at your own peril. Sgd. Able Seaman Nuisance", and hung the notice on Nuisance's bed rail. A couple of days later it was gone, filched by some souvenir hunter or oppo of Nuisance as a keepsake.

Next morning, just in time to catch the train back to Froggy Pond, the dog hopped out of bed, waited for his cap to be tied on, and licked the face of his temporary bed-mate, warning him it was time to wake up. When the man finally sat up he noticed to his amazement that he was lying on the floor. Then, seeing the massive dog standing over him, he let out a yell, and had to be calmed down by other ratings. Apparently it was the first night he'd been in the Cape Peninsula and knew nothing about Nuisance who, having sensed that the scared rating had suffered enough, sat on his haunches and held out his right paw for the rotund sailor to shake, which he did after Nuisance's oppos had explained this was the animal's usual manner of saying, "Sorry, oppo."

The Great Dane loped out of the club after another sailor had tied his cap on, just in time to catch the early train back to base, while the fat victim was complaining to the club manager that if young lions were kept as pets they should be chained up, not allowed to roam loose – one night some poor sod would get eaten alive.

Nuisance's attitude towards young children was both affectionate and docile. Whenever he happend to bump his huge frame against a youngster on his many wanderings through Simon's Town and Cape Town, he would stop and offer a paw to be shaken.

Curiously, unlike a lot of adults who came across Nuisance for the first time, the large majority of children would be neither awed nor frightened by the sheer physical size of the Great Dane. They had an instinctive feeling that this dog would protect rather than harm them in any way.

Author's Note . . .
The dialogue in this chapter was provided in an interview I had with ex-Leading Seaman G. Clark (later Petty Officer Clark during his 22 years loyal service with the Royal Navy). He now lives at Fareham, near Portsmouth, Hampshire, in the UK. Of course, he explained that this dialogue should not be taken as strictly accurate but he has an excellent memory, which I proved by asking him several questions which he answered correctly. I also asked the manager of the Union Jack Club in early 1943 about the affair of the stout sailor being turfed out of bed. He recalled it in every detail and confessed that he still chuckled when he recalled the incident.

One of the Air Force maintenance crew happened to be present at the club that same night, and it was he who informed me of the humorous episode, knowing that I was curious about events that had happened to Nuisance before I arrived at Wingfield.

Just Nuisance and matelot companion, in St George's Street, Simon's Town.

Dog-Watch!

I concede that certain incidents related here are not in chronological sequence. The explanation is simple. I have received letters from people in the Peninsula who were personally involved in these issues, but are themselves not sure what month or even in what year they occurred. This is not surprising after more than 40 years. In fact it is remarkable that they are able to recall so many details so clearly.

Several of these correspondents mentioned the occasion when Nuisance was reported run over by a car in one of Cape Town's suburbs and had been taken, badly injured, to the mine-sweeping depot at the Cape Town Docks. (Leslie M. Steyn reports in his booklet, *Just Nuisance*, how he himself was informed at his office of this accident, though I have no idea why this should have been so.)

The Dockyard CO obtained Benjamin Chaney's address and contacted him. Also the CO of *HMS Afrikander 1* (Commander Shakespear) was telephoned. A veterinary surgeon agreed to visit the depot immediately to give medical aid. Commander Shakespear and Chaney sped to the depot in the naval officer's car, and a pass was arranged for the vet when he arrived.

By the time news of Nuisance's accident had spread round *Afrikander* and Froggy Pond, and the dog's condition was critical. There were many pairs of moist eyes among the ratings, especially among the Great Dane's oppos in Hut One, Froggy Pond.

By this time Mr Chaney had arrived in the building in which the dog lay, the animal was dead, but though a Great Dane it wasn't Nuisance, though it resembled the canine AB. It was smaller and had none of the distinguishing scars on the body.

The dog's previous owner made many phone calls all over town, to *Afrikander* and Froggy Pond, confirming this case of mistaken identity. In the naval bases resounding cheers of relief were heard. Most British Jack Tars are tough chaps, but a more sentimental body of men towards the welfare of their oppos does not exist in the world.

Where Nuisance actually was during this furore has never been recorded, but it must have been somewhere other than in naval bases or the docks of Cape Town or Simon's Town, otherwise the supposed accident would have been refuted immediately.

One rating — who was in the master-at-arms' office at *HMS Afrikander I*, having violated some naval regulation at the time that news of Nuisance's death reached that office — afterward swore that the face of this iron disciplinarian sagged and tears appeared in his eyes. Two other tough ratings of the regulating staff who were present were also moist-eyed.

It was obvious that the MAA was deeply moved, because he yelled at the naval rating waiting to be booked: "Get the hell out of here and don't . . . well come back." This story was all round in a few hours as it was the only time the senior warrant officer had let anyone "off the hook" for contravention of Rules since he'd first arrived at the base.

The rating obeyed the old salt's order with alacrity.

Two hours later the ratings of *Afrikander* were personally informed over the base's internal Tannoy system that it was not Nuisance who had been killed. A degree of jubilation never equalled before or since at the camp spread among the ratings.

That evening Nuisance arrived back in the billet at Froggy Pond looking bedraggled and tired (most of his oppos saying he'd obviously been visiting one of his many lady-friends) and he was greeted with so many hugs and affectionate pats that he must have wondered what all the fuss was about. In spite of his tiredness he was led to the galley where the chief cook had "borrowed some spare rations" and fed him with a big plateful of grilled chops washed down with a quart of lager. Some of the ratings wanted to take Nuisance to town for a "thrash", but Leading Seaman Clark vetoed this and led the tired AB to his bunk, removed his cap and collar, then tucked him into his berth.

Many of Nuisance's oppos did visit town and got sloshed, and some of them who returned by the last train were booked by the guardroom staff as "returning on board one of His Majesty's ships, being drunk and not fit for duty".

Next day when they appeared before the officer of the day for punishment they all gave as their excuse that they had got drunk because, in their eyes, Nuisance had risen from the dead.

The usual punishment for this offence was seven days stoppage of leave and pay but, to their amazement, they were let off with a caution.

Two of the ratings were from Nuisance's hut and, when they informed Leading Seaman Clark how leniently they'd been treated, the big seaman grinned, and remarked that he'd no proof but he thought the old man (the CO) had whispered a quiet word in the OOD's ear before the offenders appeared before him, suggesting that the ratings had a damned good reason for celebration and to go easy on them.

Nuisance was looking his old self once more. The leading seaman had given him a shower, brushed his hairy coat till it shone and had also seen that he'd had a good breakfast. Also the killick had been busy all morning getting rid of other ratings who'd called at the hut to welcome Nuisance back home again.

The CO and MAA had paid a most unexpected visit and shaken Nuisance's paw and it was plain that both of these officers had been delighted to see the dog. The CO, in fact, had said: "Leading Seaman Clark, I would appreciate it if in future someone, a rating, of course, would accompany Nuisance on shore leave. We want no repetitions of the shock we had yesterday.''

"Aye, aye sir, consider it done." The big killick grinned as the CO left.

That night, when Nuisance returned from his usual run ashore, he was surprised that as he went outside for his hygienic nightly ablutions all the ratings from his billet gathered at the hut door to greet him. From the grins on the faces of his oppos he must have sensed their more-than-usual degree of affection. His tail wagged frantically with pleasure and his crowning moment of glory came when half a dozen of them lifted him up, carried him to his bunk and tucked him comfortably beneath the blankets. Shortly afterwards, the hut lights were switched out and every rating in the room shouted, "Good-night, Nuisance."

Nuisance responded in the only way he knew how, lifting his head off the pillow and emitting one bark that sounded like the salute of a warship's fifteen-inch gun.

In early 1941 Britain's war effort was at a very low ebb, except for the Middle East where General Wavell with his combined force of British and Commonwealth soldiers, including thousands of South African troops, had the previous year inflicted a crushing defeat on the Italians. But now the German troops had arrived in the desert, and were inflicting a series of defeats on our forces. Britain too was suffering, her main ports and cities the target of hundreds of German Luftwaffe bombers. Food in the UK was strictly rationed, German U-Boats were sinking a large percentage of merchant ships bringing supplies to the UK.

The reader may wonder what this has to do with Nuisance, but indirectly it was to affect his life in many ways. Ships which used to sail directly for the Mediterranean were now being directed round the Cape of Good Hope to the Suez Canal, reducing the catastrophic loss of Royal Navy and Merchant Navy ships sunk by the Germans and Italians in the Straits of Gibraltar and the island of Malta seaways.

This meant that Cape Town and Simon's Town were now visited by many more naval ships than previously, with the inevitable influx of thousands more British naval men to these ports.

About this time Ajax, Nuisance's canine civilian oppo, was run over in the street by a tram and tragically killed; but, of course, Nuisance did not know this. On his few visits to the United Services Institute in Simon's Town, he would greet Benjamin Chaney with his usual friendliness, then prowl the whole area looking for his canine chum, the bulldog.

Chaney would watch Nuisance's futile search with sympathy and sadness.

Then Nuisance committed three offences contrary to Admiralty Rules and Regulations — unfortunately all within a week of one another.

Like all British naval ratings serving on ships or bases throughout the world, all ranks above that of ordinary seamen were allowed all-night leave, usually from 5 p.m. to 7 a.m. the next morning. (Ordinary seamen had to report back to their ships or bases by midnight the same day) One evening Nuisance had visited his previous owner in the Institute at Simon's

Town, where he was royally dined and had a quart of lager.

He then proceeded to the Prince Albert Hotel where he received a loving welcome from his Great Dane girl-friend, and a few more pints of lager from Judy's owner, who was the landlord and very fond of Nuisance.

He could sup an amazing amount of beer without showing signs that he'd been drinking alcohol at all so, still steady on his feet, he made for *HMS Afrikander I.*

He was duly passed through the guardroom with a few friendly pats and made straight for the ratings' galley where there was always a tasty snack set out for him. On arriving at the back door he loudly scratched the wooden panels rather than give his lion-like bark and so wake up most of the sleeping ratings. After all, it was one o'clock in the morning and he also knew there were a few vacant beds in a small dormitory annexe of the galley.

A minute later one of the cook-house ratings opened the door, greeted him fondly, took him to a spare bunk, removed his cap and collar then tucked him up snugly in the bed. At six o'clock the next morning he was roused by the same rating who led Nuisance into the galley where the chief cook and his helpers were preparing breakfasts.

The Chief heated up three large steak-and-kidney pies which Nuisance hungrily gulped down, followed by a quart of milk from a saucepan. Then the Chief noticed the time, it was 6.30, and grabbed one of his assistants and told him to take Nuisance on the double to the main gates. The lorry for Froggy Pond left *Afrikander* at that time.

When Nuisance and the breathless rating arrived at the gate the vehicle was disappearing down the road, but one of *Afrikander's* guardroom staff pointed Nuisance after it, telling him to run and catch it up.

Nuisance took no notice, ambling off and plainly fed up at having to walk to Froggy Pond. It wasn't Nuisance's lucky day. When he did get to Froggy Pond the CO, paying a routing visit to the guardhouse, noticed the time was 7.45 and told the regulating petty officer in charge to report Nuisance as being 45 minutes adrift. He would have to appear before *HMS Afrikander I's* CO in answer to this charge — after appearing before the officer-of-the-day at Froggy Pond at nine o'clock that morning, who would then refer him to a more superior officer for punishment.

A charge of being "adrift", or absent without leave, was considered by the Navy to be a more serious offence than the Army and Royal Air Force regarded it. The explanation is logical. A shore base is regarded as a ship. If any member of a ship's crew is absent at the time he is stipulated to return, in theory the ship could have sailed short of one member of the crew. If the ship encountered enemy forces, that absentee could possibly affect the performance of that ship and, in turn, contribute to a defeat. Therefore, to be adrift was considered by the Royal Navy as having let down not only the ship and other members of the crew, but the whole fleet of which he was a part.

At nine o'clock that morning Nuisance found himself escorted by a regulating petty officer to the admin block where, in the corridor, two other ratings were waiting as they had also been adrift that morning, The petty officer was holding Nuisance by the collar, but had to let go as the dog was fed up already by the proceedings and preferred to lie down on the corridor floor. The first rating went in and came out five minutes later and said to his oppo, as he went by, that he had been remanded for punishment by *Afrikander's* CO. The other rating went in and received the same sentence.

Then it was Nuisance's turn.

What happened in the OOD's office has not been recorded and all that is known about the interview is what the regulating petty officer told Leading Seaman Clark when he took Nuisance back to his billet, and the leading seaman roared with laughter as the PO described Nuisance's conduct after entering the office.

The OOD was a young sub-lieutenant who had the master-at-arms by his side. As the MAA read out the charge Nuisance sat on his haunches and assumed a begging position. The young officer grinned and the grim-faced warrant officer chided his superior, saying this was no joke. The young sub-lieutenant asked the MAA if he could deliver a "caution" and not put Nuisance on the CO's report, as this was the canine AB's first offence. But the strict disciplinarian, though he liked Nuisance, was a stickler for correct procedure against any offender, and pointed out that two other ratings had been remanded for punishment by *Afrikander's* CO, and they had been only 15 minutes adrift.

The young officer had no alternative but to place Nuisance on the CO's list.

Nuisance, who'd had his cap removed when the order "off caps" had been given on first entering the office, dropped back to all fours as the PO tied his cap back on. All the above events were detailed to the leading seaman by the regulating petty officer, who also said that the killick had been designated by the MAA to accompany Nuisance to *Afrikander* to appear before the CO in four days' time at nine in the morning.

Four days later Leading Seaman Clark went with Nuisance in a lorry to *HMS Afrikander*, arriving about 8.45, and reported to the master-at-arms office. The MAA informed the killick that the CO had decided that Nuisance should set another precedent, as offenders who were to appear before the CO for his jurisdiction did so in strict alphabetical order of their surname's first letter. In other words, if one of the offenders had a surname beginning with "A" he took priority. As "N" was down the alphabetic sequence, he should have been one of the last to appear. As the leading seaman led Nuisance to the admin block and down the corridor towards the CO's office there were at least a dozen other ratings lounging there waiting for their CO's decisions, punishments, or charges dismissed.

Promptly at nine the MAA opened the CO's door from the inside, poked his head out and shouted:

"Able Seaman Nuisance and escort, quick march for CO's report."

The leading seaman led Nuisance into the office. The CO of *Afrikander* was seated behind a large desk, on his right hand the CO of Froggy Pond stood, while the MAA was on his left, carrying a wooden clipboard on which were pinned the charge sheets. The CO had Nuisance's service documents lying open on the top of the desk. Nuisance attempted to sit down, but his escort pulled him to all fours, and the dog stood facing his accusers, long tongue hanging out of his mouth and tail wagging furiously.

(An account of these proceedings follows, although as ex-Petty Officer Clark explained when I interviewed him last year, the words cannot possibly be verbatim, but he well remembers the gist of this dialogue, which I quote as he related.)

The MAA looked at his clipboard and then ordered:

"Able Seaman Nuisance, off caps."

The dog's escort removed Nuisance's cap and held it in his right hand.

The MAA continued:

"Able Seaman Nuisance you are hereby charged that on the morning of *(ex-Petty Officer Clark cannot remember the date or month, but is adamant it was in the year 1941)* you did return aboard Froggy Pond at 0745 hours, being 45 minutes adrift. Witnesses to this were the guardroom PO and the CO of Froggy Pond — how do you plead?"

Nuisance yawned hugely, he was 'chocker' with the whole affair. The CO placed a hand over his mouth as if to hide a smile, and then said (he was well-known for having a strong sense of humour), glancing at Nuisance's service documents as he spoke: "I do not have any doubts this rating is guilty as charged, especially as his CO was present when he returned, and I think it rather fortunate that this rating cannot enter a plea of guilty or not guilty as, having heard him give voice on various occasions, I want to be in a position to hear what the other defaulters have to say, not half-deaf. You, Master, will therefore enter a plea of guilty on behalf of this able-seaman."

"Aye, aye sir," replied the MAA.

Nuisance's tail was now wagging furiously and the CO could no longer conceal a smile as he continued:

"There are, however, extenuating circumstances in this case. On the morning he was adrift the chief petty officer cook at Froggy Pond rang the MAA here at *Afrikander* claiming this rating missed the bus from that base only because the chief cook at *Afrikander* had overlooked the time and so caused the defendant to miss the bus. Is that correct MAA?"

"That is correct sir, our chief cook says he is willing to accept all blame for this offence."

"That speaks very well for the chief cook's loyalty to this rating but does not excuse the offence. All ratings are personally responsible for not being adrift. As this is a first offence, I am going to let this rating off with a caution and it is not to be entered on his conduct sheet. However any repetition of a like offence will be dealt with severely. Able Seaman Nuisance is dismissed with a caution."

The MAA barked out:

"Able Seaman Nuisance, the CO's punishment is a caution and case dismissed. On caps. About turn, quick march."

The CO spoke again:

"Leading Seaman Clark, stand fast. Master-at-Arms, would you please take Nuisance outside and leave him with one of the ratings, then return here."

As the MAA took the dog out of the office, the CO said:

"Leading Seaman Clark, I just wanted a word or two about Nuisance. I understand he is in your billet and under your charge?"

"Yes sir, he's a wonderful animal, every one of the lads is as fond of him as I am."

The CO looked thoughtfully at the big killick, then remarked:

"I expect you're wondering why I didn't award Nuisance the usual punishment for being adrift which as you know, often means stoppage of leave and pay for seven days — and double that for persistent offenders. As you are the only rating to ever have charge of an officially-enlisted dog in the Royal Navy, I feel it only right to explain why I awarded only a caution.

"First there were extenuating circumstances. Secondly, your CO at Froggy Pond informs me that Nuisance has created a more friendly attitude between personnel stationed there than he has ever known, and is no trouble at all. Now, in confidence Leading Seaman Clark, has there been any bother in the billet with respect to Nuisance?"

The big seaman thought a moment before answering but, knowing the CO of *Afrikander* was noted for his sense of justice, explained about the incident between Nuisance and the drunken rating, emphasizing that the man thought the world of the Great Dane — even more so after realising Nuisance could have killed him.

The CO had listened intently and said: "I think that seaman was very fortunate, if he hadn't been one of the dog's friends I hate to think what might have happened. You wouldn't like Nuisance transferred to another billet then?"

The leading seaman was horrified at the suggestion and said appealingly: "Don't do that sir, my lads would probably start a mutiny, or put in requests for a transfer to whatever billet he was put in."

"I have no intention of doing so leading seaman, but there is one problem. Your CO informs me that he has recommended you for up-rating to petty officer in six months time and I have endorsed it, so you can take it as an established fact that your promotion will be approved. That will mean your leaving the billet to shift quarters to the petty officers' mess. Will the new leading seaman be able to cope with Nuisance?"

"Thanks very much about my promotion sir, and I'll not deny leaving

46

the dog will take most of my pleasure from it, but Nuisance will be OK with whoever's in charge of him — that is, begging your pardon sir, someone in "square rig". You see, sir, the dog regards everyone in that rig as an oppo — though it's not true he thinks everyone in fore-and-aft rig is a kind of enemy — it's just that he doesn't like them much. Probably that's because when Mr Chaney was his owner most lads who went in the Institute at Simon's Town were ratings, who spoiled him when he was younger and he's not forgot that. But he has no favourites, we had a new ordinary seaman billeted in our hut last week, someone he'd never known before, and Nuisance spends as much time with him as others in the billet who've been his oppos for months."

The CO smiled.

"Thanks very much for that information, leading seaman. I must admit Nuisance has never shown much respect for officers' ranks when I've been present, but no one will ever be able to accuse him of being an officer's pet. Alright leading seaman, dismissed."

The seaman stiffened to attention, noticing as he did so that even the MAA was smiling with approval at him. If the senior warrant officer showed even slight appreciation of a rating his future months at Froggy Pond (unless he did something stupid) would be made more pleasant for being regarded by the MAA as an excellent killick.

He went outside, took Nuisance's collar in his hand and walked towards the galley — after a narrow escape like that Nuisance needed sustenance.

The chief cook, on hearing of Nuisance's dismissal from punishment by the CO, laid on a good meal for the dog and his usual quart of milk. At mid-day when all ratings showed up in the hut at Froggy Pond, anxious to know how Nuisance had fared with the CO, they cheered when told what had happened. Once more the Great Dane found himself the recipient of pats and strokes from his oppos.

He made for his bunk but, on observing his mates trooping through the door to the galley for dinner, decided he was still hungry and followed them. After dinner when they got back in the hut a messenger from the base's office was there.

He had an official warrant card from the SAR in his hand — a cardboard season ticket for free train rides.

The killick, remembering the watch card incident, fastened it right up to the steel ring so Nuisance couldn't get his teeth to it and asked the other ratings to put the collar out of Nuisance's reach when they removed it at any time when the dog wanted to kip, so he could not chew up this valuable free pass.

A week later, the bombshell burst. As the Tannoy blared "Wakey, wakey", a chief petty officer walked into the hut, and passed Leading Seaman Clark a flimsy slip of paper. The big seaman read it, then rolled it into a ball, flung it down the centre of the room and whirled angrily on the CPO, yelling:

"Bloodyhell, whose idea is this then chief? It's cruelty, that dog's got to know everybody at this camp. Why only last week the CO at *Afrikander* practically promised me on his bloody oath Nuisance would be staying in this billet.''

The CPO looked at Nuisance, who was just slithering from his bunk, and turned a sad expression towards the big seaman, saying:

"Sorry killick, I'm just as upset about this as you are, all I know is this signal came in from *Afrikander's* CO last night. Nuisance is to be transferred there first thing this morning — and I have a lorry outside waiting to take him there."

The rest of the ratings in the hut had listened to the chief's words in disbelief, then with a great sense of sadness and dismay. The rating whose bed was next to Nuisance's was fastening his collar round the massive neck, then reached down the dog's cap from a high shelf and, with tears in his eyes, tied the cap on top of Nuisance's head. In fact there wasn't a dry eye in the hut, including the Chief's, when he realised the emotion with which these tough seamen had greeted his news.

Then Nuisance saw one of his oppos rolling up his mattress, blanket and pillow and his mind was intelligent enough to grasp that something unusual was happening, especially when the CPO took a leash from the killick and clipped it to his collar.

All his oppos lined up down one side of the hut and the big leading seaman led Nuisance to each one where he lifted up Nuisance's paw to be shaken by each billet mate. Then the killick (with eyes suspiciously moist) took the dog over towards the CPO and asked:

"Come on chief, be a mate, you must have some idea why Nuisance is being transferred, what's the gen?"

The chief looked at the big seaman and answered:

"All I know killick, is that the CO at *Afrikander* is being invited all over the place round Simon's Town and Cape Town, to speak at functions which will help the war effort. Nuisance has become a sort of hero, even to civilians, and the CO plans to take him as company to these do's. Not all the time, perhaps only one a week. Nuisance will enjoy himself, there'll be lashings of grub and lager for him. Tell you another thing, the CO here nearly went crazy when he heard; says, if it's the last thing he does, he's going to get Nuisance back here in a few weeks."

Leading Seaman Clark felt a bit happier at this news, perhaps the parting would last only a month or so, and they'd be able to see the dog when he went ashore to Cape Town.

Then the chief led the dog to the door and, as they went out, Nuisance turned and faced his oppos, lifted up his head, floppy ears pointed, his large damp pug nose flared, lifted his right paw, then barked one lionlike roar. Many of his oppos declared afterwards that every window in the hut shook and rattled.

Probably an exaggeration, like so many stories concerning the canine AB, but then tall stories were only commensurate with the dog's huge size and almost human intelligence. . . .

As the chief and Nuisance reached the lorry Froggy Pond's CO met them, bent down and held out his hand for the dog to shake, speaking to his most popular AB in the base. Nuisance hesitated for a moment — after all this man was dressed in fore and aft rig, therefore not one of his oppos — but some inherent animal sense must have taken over and made the dog realise that this man was very fond of him, so he reciprocated the kindness and held out his paw. The CO shook and patted his head, even opening the back canvas cover of the vehicle for the Chief and Nuisance to climb inside.

As the lorry reached the gates of Froggy Pond guardroom even three of the regulating staff emerged and waved a farewell to Nuisance, whose head stuck out of the canvas sheet looking backwards.

On arrival at *HMS Afrikander I* Nuisance was led into the guardroom and a rating on duty there was instructed to take the dog to his new quarters.

When Nuisance was shown into his billet, he looked curiously around, the large head taking in the surroundings. These huts were bigger than those at Froggy Pond and had more bunks lined down each side of the walls. The rating showed Nuisance to one of the bunks and pointed to it. The Great Dane understood at once — this was his bed. He jumped on the bunk, stretched out his large frame, the hind paws nearly touching the base, and put his head on the pillow.

There was only one occupant in the hut besides the dog and guardroom rating, a "sweeper", a rating excused all duties outside the billet so he could sweep the floor, wash down the windows and generally keep the room spotless.

The guardroom rating had a few words with the sweeper, then left. The sweeper approached Nuisance, lying on the bunk, untied his cap and laid it on the bed's locker top. The dog was preparing for a kip, occasionally opening one eye to make sure nothing was likely to disturb him, and dropped off to sleep, the great chest slowly rising and deflating as he breathed.

An hour or so passed and then the door opened and a small leading seaman entered the billet, and anyone who heard him speak could tell that his dialect was cockney.

The sweeper jerked his thumb at the sleeping dog:

"I've been in the Cape only a few days killick, but I've already heard tales about Nuisance there. Didn't believe half of them, but I do now, especially about his size. There's a touch of lion in him and that's no error. He's a real old hand, no sooner than he gets here than he's in his kip. By the way, the CO wants him in his office at 11 this morning; guardroom rating said you was to take him in there, wearing his cap."

The diminutive leading seaman grinned.

"I know all about that chum, the master-at-arms nailed me about ten minutes ago; he also gave me this dog-brush. Nuisance is to be brushed every morning after breakfast, I'll do that." The leading seaman woke up Nuisance about 10.45; shined him up, tied on his cap and set off for the admin block.

Promptly at 11 the leading seaman knocked on the CO's door. The rating led Nuisance inside, stood at attention and said:

"Leading Seaman Brown sir, reporting with Able Seaman Nuisance as ordered."

The CO sat behind his desk, two other officers seated each side of him, the MAA standing directly behind them. The CO said: "I asked you to bring Nuisance here Brown, so I could explain my reasons for transferring him from Froggy Pond. Primarily, I am constantly receiving invitations from prominent citizens of the Peninsula to attend gatherings connected with helping South Africa's war effort. Many of them ask if Nuisance can accompany me.

"I cannot possibly accept all of them, my other duties preclude that. However, my number one (second-in-command)," indicating the lieutenant commander on his right, "will accept various requests, and appear as my representative. Your divisional officer and, incidentally, Nuisance's too," pointing to the other officer, "and the MAA are present to hear my instructions regarding Nuisance.

"As to hygiene, Nuisance is as clean in his bodily functions as any human being, probably cleaner. This you will observe for yourself, but he does like a shower every day and a good rub down and brush-up. This is your responsibility. I am putting you in charge of this AB, and when I attend any charity functions with Nuisance you will accompany me, to prevent him living up to his name. He will not be assigned any watch and will be free to go ashore every day at the same time as other ratings.

"You will see that he takes his meals in the galley, at meal-times. The chief cook has already been given instructions about his diet. If any problems crop up regarding this rating report them promptly to the MAA who will inform me.

"Look after him well — he is regarded with a great deal of affection by citizens around the Cape besides the respect accorded him by his naval colleagues. Understood Brown?"

"Aye, aye sir, understood," replied the little leading seaman.

In spite of his lack of height the leading seaman was tremendously broad across his shoulders, and powerful, which several of his oppos had learnt to their cost when taunting him about his short frame. By this time Nuisance was chocker by having to stand there and, suddenly, lay down in front of his CO.

The leading seaman tried to lift him to his feet with the short leash he held in one hand, which was clipped to Nuisance's collar, but the Great Dane resisted his efforts and gave a wide yawn. The CO stood up, looked down at the sprawled AB and laughed.

"It seems he's had enough orders for one day Brown, and also showing disrespect for his CO. That's all leading seaman, except for just one thing. When he appears on the base he is to wear cap and collar at all times. When he retires to his bunk remove them both. Dismissed."

The leading seaman left the office with Nuisance trotting contentedly beside him, tail wagging furiously, and they made their way to the galley.

Here, the chief cook welcomed Nuisance like a long-lost brother and laid on a banquet of meaty bones that even quenched Nuisance's usually insatiable appetite. He even left half the quart of milk put down for him, gave a whine of appreciation, and followed his killick towards the billet. Once inside, the leading seaman removed his hat and collar while the dog walked unerringly to the bunk he'd been allocated, leapt up, laid his head on the pillow, gave a great yawn and in five minutes was fast asleep.

Suddenly there was a loud knock on the door and the sweeper opened it. A rating poked his head inside and asked if he and some of this oppos could say hello to Nuisance, having just heard of the canine AB's arrival. The killick walked to the door and looked out. There were about 50 ratings waiting there to greet Nuisance, so the killick quietly closed the door and spoke to them.

"Nuisance has got his head down, mates, but he'll be going ashore tonight in Cape Town. Best thing you can do is to meet him at Simon's Town railway station, he'll probably be glad to see all of you. . . . One word of warning though, if any of you wear fore-and-aft rig, don't expect much joy from Nuisance, he's strictly a square-rig oppo."

There was a murmer of agreement from the assembled ratings and they wandered off.

When the other ratings came into the billet before going to lunch they gathered excitedly round the sleeping AB, the leading seaman begging them not to make too much noise — an oppo didn't wake up a mate unless absolutely necessary.

Nuisance slept till 4.30 that afternoon, by which time most ratings billeted in the room had arrived. Nuisance raised his head from the pillow, gave a happy yawn and leapt out of bed — he guessed it was time for another meal. The killick tied on the dog's cap and collar, then lined up all the ratings, led Nuisance down the room where he shook hands with his new mess-mates. The hound then walked towards the door, ran to the perimeter fence about a hundred metres away where no buildings were in the vicinity and, watched by his new mates, dug a deep hole in the ground and squatted. When finished, front paws scratching frantically, he filled in the hole, ran a few yards, lowered his hindquarters and dragged his backside along the ground, then headed back to the billet. He stopped outside and his broad tongue then licked all four paws before entering. One rating muttered with awe, "I'll be buggered, never seen a dog do that before; that bloody Nuisance is cleaner than a stoker."

It wasn't the first time this comparison had been made . . . .

After tea and another huge meal, Nuisance made his way to Simon's Town station which was packed with ratings, most of them determined to meet the canine matelot.

There were many cries of "Here, Nuisance" from ratings waiting for the train and the dog trotted up and down the platform, offering his paw, but never stopped longer with one rating than another. He had no favourites.

Even though Leading Seaman Brown was on the platform, who had been with Nuisance all day, the dog's greeting to him was no longer or more affectionate than that he displayed to other ratings.

As the train for Cape Town drew into the station Nuisance, having the advantage of four legs compared to his human oppos' two, was first aboard and took up his usual three seats by a window. Several ratings could not find vacant seats, but such was the respect in which Nuisance was held, not one of the standing seamen thought of asking Nuisance to make room for them.

They'd rather have walked to town than do this.

After the train reached Cape Town and a horde of sailors made for the exits, Nuisance attached himself to a pair of ratings who were walking towards the open-air market near the station. The two mates were delighted with his company and strolled in the direction of the city hall. They entered a canteen or café known as Mayor's Garden which many sailors, soldiers and airmen frequented, owing to the cheap prices, and the excellent cookery.

All the cooks and waitresses were unpaid volunteers, similar to the Womens' Voluntary Services in the UK, and they made a fuss of their canine visitor although he'd been there before, laying down a big dish of cutlets for him.

At one end of the dining room was a stage with a settee on it and, after his meal, Nuisance sauntered towards it then stretched out, denying anyone else the privilege.

Also on the stage was a piano at which a man was playing dance tunes. There was a cleared space and many of the young waitresses acted as partners to any of the customers who requested a dance. This particular evening Nuisance must have been feeling a bit lively and, after watching several couples dancing round the floor, sprang down from the settee and walked over to one young lady who happened to be on the entertainment committee.

The pianist was playing a waltz, and as Nuisance stood near this girl, she jokingly asked him to dance.

She never for a moment expected him to accept. Nuisance's attitude to all females (other than children) was a degree or two lower than that he accorded to sailors who wore fore-and-aft rig. However, this time his tail wagged furiously and to everyone's amazement Nuisance reared up on his hind legs, placed his two front paws on each of her shoulders, and off they went in perfect time to the music.

Many years later (in 1984 to be exact) this lady wrote to the *Cape Times* describing this experience. "I was only 5ft 2in in height and Nuisance towered over me, but off we went in correct waltz time — 1, 2, 3 — and he even guided me by putting pressure on a shoulder to indicate which way he wanted me to turn. I was a ballroom dancer, but that waltz was one of the best I ever had . . . what a beautiful memory.''

This event is probably one of the least plausible truths in this book, but there is indisputable proof that this occurred.

What the young lady does not recount in her article is the tremendous roar of applause made by all present when the dance finished — and the dog held out his paw for an encore. The latter information was obtained from Leading Seaman Brown, who was told about it by one of the actual ratings who took Nuisance to that canteen.

For any other readers who doubt the veracity of Nuisance's dance at the canteen the lady's name is Mrs Girlie Baker who wrote to the chief reporter of the *Cape Times,* Roger Williams. An article appeared in that newspaper written by the lady personally on May 15, 1984.

Next day Nuisance's ability as a ballroom dancer was the talk of all *HMS Afrikander I's* ship's company.

At noon meal-time the comedian (and there was invariably one such character in most rating's messes, and officers' wardrooms as well) attempted to persuade Nuisance to repeat his dancing performance. However the canine AB wasn't in the mood — he'd dance only when he felt like it and not at the whim of any rating, even a mess-deck oppo.

The would-be comedian persisted in his efforts to such an extent that Nuisance turned nasty, his upper jowls wrinkled, his tail stuck out (no wagging) and there was a menacing rumble of anger.

Leading Seaman Brown, at the other end of the room, shouted: "Leave Nuisance alone you stupid bastard, that dog's about ready to rip your bloody silly face. If he does turn on you there'll be a new patient in the sick-bay in about a minute, or a corpse in the mortuary at the side of it. Now bloody well pack it in, or I'll fill you in myself."

The comic instantly obeyed and quickly retreated to his own bunk.

The dog's tail started wagging again, the snarls petered out and Nuisance walked to his bed, yawned and lay down, waiting till it was time for his next meal.

Out on the town! An unidentified Royal Navy warrant officer has his picture taken in a Cape Town pub — with one of the pub's best-known "regulars" — Able Seaman Just Nuisance.

Every dog has his day

As the months of 1941 rolled by, several incidents occurred which confirmed the growing wisdom of Nuisance and his increasing intelligence. His most enjoyable times were the week-ends — Saturdays and Sundays when all ratings not on duty were granted what is known in the Navy as seven-bell leave.

Even at naval shore bases a ship's bell of some kind was hung, usually near the guardroom. This bell was rung to mark the passing hours. Midnight was eight bells; half an hour later, one dong of the bell; one o'clock in the morning two dongs; and so on. One more ring of the bell added every half hour, till the time was four o'clock, which would be eight bells again. The whole process was repeated throughout the day, except between four and eight when the usual four-hour watch was shortened to two hours each, called first dog watch and second dog watch respectively.

Therefore, ratings were allowed ashore from mid-day on Saturdays and Sundays till 7,30 the next morning, which was seven bells. Thus the term seven-bell leave.

Every time the ship's bell sounded in *Afrikander* Nuisance would perk up his ears. I am not suggesting that he could determine the hours these bells denoted, but he had an uncanny instinct for knowing how many rings described the times for shore leave.

One of the surgeon-lieutenants at *Afrikander* who'd studied psychology had an interesting theory which he expounded to Leading Seaman Brown, who had visited the sick-bay to have a boil on his neck lanced.

When the naval doctor learnt that Brown was in charge of Nuisance he remarked: "You know what my theory is for the astounding intelligence that dog has, Brown?"

"I've no idea sir, but it *is* a fact that Nuisance is almost human in his thinking", replied the leading seaman.

"Exactly, Brown, that's my whole point. Most dogs have only one master or mistress, and few are allowed to sleep in their owner's room."

"Now Nuisance is in the company of sailors every day; he's even with them when they go ashore, and sleeps and eats with them. He's with humans all the time, and it's logical to believe that he has gradually absorbed some of a human's intellect. Of course he'll never attain the brainpower of a man, that's impossible, but as time goes on and you chaps teach him certain things, he'll be even more intelligent than he is now, certainly far more clever than the ordinary dog. Do you understand my reasoning, Brown?"

"Yes sir, and I think what you say makes good sense," Brown replied.

Invariably at week-ends, Nuisance would be the first to arrive on the platform at Simon's Town station just after noon. This was the advantage his four legs gave him over other ratings, the ability to run much faster than they could.

After arriving in Cape Town, Nuisance's first call would be at a hotel on Adderley Street called The Standard, but which most of his oppos referred to as the Texas Bar, because its entrance had batwing type doors like those seen in saloons in American cowboy films. The manager of the Texas Bar and his staff regarded Nuisance as their best customer. Though this patron of the premises never paid for his first drink, this always being on the house — that is, the manager always poured a quart of Lion lager into a large brass bowl for the dog to imbibe — he knew that when word got round to other sailors in town that Nuisance was at his hotel, ratings would flock there.

Perhaps the reason Nuisance liked this hotel best was that the swinging doors allowed him to nudge them with the great canine head and enter, whereas at most other hotels the dog had to wait for someone to open the more robust doors.

By the time Nuisance had quaffed his first quart of lager, there'd be a dozen sailors waiting to buy him another. But Nuisance had now learnt to exercise caution in how much beer he drank at any one time, after suffering several monumental hangovers from over-indulgence of his favourite tipple.

He would accept only a couple more quarts bought by his oppos, and would then make his way up the stairs which led to an open-air balcony overlooking Adderley Street. This balcony had several tables and chairs where customers could enjoy their drinks and a view of the main street. The vantage point allowed them to watch passers-by and public transport vehicles making their way in both directions.

Nuisance would approach the guard rails of the balcony, rear up on his hind legs, place his fore-paws on the horizontal rail top, and enjoy the scene below.

If he saw any other dogs on the pavements parading by, most of them on leashes held by their owners, Nuisance's tail would swing in double time. He would give one ear-splitting bark, which wasn't too bad on other peoples' eardrums as the roar took place in the open, but nevertheless every face in the street cast a look in the direction of the balcony. Many of the citizens who knew Nuisance by sight (and sound) laughed and smiled at the canine AB. If he didn't see other dogs, no bark was necessary. He simply wanted to let other canines know he was present — and far above them in all respects . . . .

Nuisance would remain in this position for half an hour or so, then make his way down the stairs, out of the hotel and head for the dockyard at the lower end of Adderley Street. The guards at the entrance had instructions from the senior officer to admit Nuisance at any time — after all, he was a Royal Navy rating with documents to prove it.

On reaching the wharf where several ships were moored, Nuisance would lift his large black nose as if sniffing the salt sea air, then gaze round the waters of Table Bay inspecting any other vessels which had anchored out in the roadstead.

Most of the ships tied up at the dockside were merchant freighters, but some of them were small naval craft, sometimes even a Royal Navy sloop. Usually however, navy ships of war would harbour in Simon's Town, which had all facilities for supplying service vessels with victuals, ammunition, torpedoes and engine spare parts and if any ratings were sick and needed hospital treatment they were brought ashore and replaced by men from *HMS Afrikander I.*

All the ships tied up at the wharf had gangways down from their decks to the pier-side, and at the foot of these gangways it was not unusual for one of the crew to be on guard to prevent unauthorised boarding. If any of these security men tried to restrict Nuisance from going aboard, there were always plenty of dockyard police handy who would have a quiet word in their ears. They explained, to the guards' bewilderment, that this monster canine was an officially-enlisted able seaman of the Royal Navy. If they wanted to check this, just look at the identity disc on the dog's collar and, incidentally, the Great Dane was also a close friend of the harbour-master.

Not many of the guards wished to examine the disc. One look at the animal's size was enough, and they allowed him to pass up the gangplanks. When Nuisance boarded a ship he had only one purpose in mind, to search out any other canines on board and rout them. Other dogs had no business on ships — that was his prerogative. Sailors formed the crews — and seamen had only one oppo, Nuisance.

The dockyard police were responsible for the rumours which abounded about Nuisance chasing ships' pet dogs, and being their executioner. It is true that he chased them — but there was no hard evidence that he'd killed any of them, though it was possible.

Some of these pets were, like their crews, tough characters. Their way of life on the high seas made them so, but the biggest dog Nuisance had ever encountered aboard one of these ships was a Labrador retriever and he looked like a whippet compared to the canine AB's mighty proportions.

Nuisance's many excursions in search of victims had provided some duty crewmen on various ships in past months with excellent entertainment. Quite a large number of the ship's pets were small pooches — terriers, spaniels, whippets and grateful mongrels being the favourites preferred by the crews. On one ship the pet was a Pekingese, whose height was 7 cm below the bone joints of Nuisance's fore paws.

In the vast majority of chases Nuisance found himself outwitted. The ship's pets may not have had the Great Dane's intelligence, but knew every corner and hiding place, both on deck and in the quarters below, so Nuisance spent many hours in futile pursuit. He would then walk off the ship with his nose in the air as if disgusted with the lack of sportsmanship displayed by his canine cousins.

Some ships had pet cats and when Nuisance became aware of this fact, his disdain reached a pinnacle. He would ignore these felines and make a wide detour round the spot where they sat, arching their backs and spitting, but backing away all the same. A cat can give a good account of itself in most fights against a dog, but Nuisance was no ordinary dog, he must have seemed like three canines built into one huge frame to these furry seafarers.

Three days after Nuisance's transfer to *Afrikander* from Froggy Pond, one evening in a hotel in Cape Town Leading Seaman Brown sat drinking lager with three of his oppos. They were discussing Nuisance, when a merchant sailor approached them and asked if the dog they were talking about was "a Great Dane big as a bloody lion."

The killick answered that it was, and he'd the honour of being put in charge of it by his CO. The dog was an officially-enlisted member of the Royal Navy, and he politely asked the Merchant Navy seaman to join their table. The man told his story.

Apparently the merchant sailor about four that afternoon had been feeding the ship's dog, a small mongrel, on deck near the gangway when he spotted a "great head rise above the gangplank, and thought at first it was a bloody lion that had escaped from some zoo in town. Then, as it came on deck, I realised it was a Great Dane, but a lot bigger than any other I'd ever seen." The mongrel noticed the canine AB and, leaving his saucerful of herrings to be eaten at a safer time of day, spun round, yapped in terror and sped off towards the nearest hatch-opening.

Unfortunately his paws slipped on a newly-hosed section of the deck and he rolled on his side.

In two bounds Nuisance was standing astride the mongrel who lay there petrified, and the huge dog lowered its jaws towards the small head. The merchant seaman confessed that he too was terrified and unable to shout for help.

In another few seconds the crew would be minus one pet. They'd have missed the little dog as he was a good 'hand' who, being so small, could reach confined spaces and kill ships rats that were a menace to hygiene in any vessel. One day he had killed 16 of these rodents in short time.

However, Nuisance had made no sound, not even a growl. Then, to the seaman's relief and stupefaction, he saw the Great Dane place one huge forepaw on the mongrel's side and roll him over on his back so that all four stumpy legs pointed skywards. Nuisance then started to lick the litle dog's ears, then its belly, the mongrel whimpering with delight. This went on for two or three minutes then the Great Dane moved to one side while the little pet got back on all four feet and licked Nuisance's forepaw, which was as high as the mongrel could reach.

The merchant sailor had got his nerve back and beckoned Nuisance to follow him. He thought it would be a good idea to show some of his ship-mates this monster dog and tell them about his antics.

The sailor entered a hatchway, Nuisance close behind him, and the mongrel at the big dog's heels. He opened a door which led into a small cabin where four of his pals were seated round a table at a game of cards. They looked at the Great Dane in astonishment. When the sailor told them about the occurrence on deck the canine AB accepted their attentions as if they were his due.

One of the sailors took hold of the small disc attached to Nuisance's collar, read it, whistled in disbelief, and told the others that this dog was an able seaman in the Royal Navy. They all looked at the disc and had to agree it was a fact.

In the cabin was a cage which held a parrot. One of his mates took off the dark cover cloth. This bird could speak only a few words.

Blinking its beady eyes the gaudy bird ducked its head and stared down at Nuisance, squawking the only words it could say.

"It's mutiny skipper; you're a right bastard; . . . you. Wakey, Wakey."

Though Nuisance had been sitting on the cabin floor, the dog jumped as if he'd been shot. His ears flicked upright, his tail stood straight out parallel to the deck and never moved. Nuisance's eyes stared at the bird and the sailor swore they had a glazed look. One ear twitched, then the

other, till both were semaphoring with the regularity of a ticking watch.

The bird kept repeating the words.

Then Nuisance's legs trembled, he rubbed one paw across his eyes and stared at the bird again as if in a trance. One of the seamen flung the dark cloth back over the cage.

Nuisance shook his head, then let out one bark and the canine hero fled from the cabin as if the devil himself was after him.

By the time the merchant seaman had finished the story about this intrepid AB, Leading Seaman Brown and his three oppos were helpless with mirth.

When the rest of Nuisance's oppos heard the story, Nuisance for the next day or two wondered why all his pals were splitting their sides . . . .

Later that day Leading Seaman Brown went round his room collecting cash from all the ratings billeted there. His intention was to go ashore that night, visit the ship on which Nuisance had his traumatic meeting with the parrot and buy the bird off the ship's crew. He collected more than £60, enough he thought to bargain with the crew members. He had no luck. The crew refused to part with the bird even for double the amount.

Letters continued to pour in from all round the Peninsula to the CO of *HMS Afrikander I* requesting his and Nuisance's presence at various charity gatherings designed to raise money for South Africa's war effort, or to recruit men and women to serve in the armed forces.

The CO had two sets of stereotyped replies prepared, and these read:

Dear Sir/Madam,

In reply to your kind invitation for me to attend the charity function along with my Commanding Officer to be held at . . . on the . . . inst, I am very sorry to refuse this request because my services on that day are needed by the Royal Navy.

As I cannot read or write, my CO has kindly dictated this letter on my behalf and please do not hesitate to ask for my presence at any future date as, by that time, my rigorous duties may have decreased, allowing me to attend.

I send you a copy of my Service Documents so you may display them at this function, but my CO wishes to point out to everyone concerned that the Commander-in-Chief, South Atlantic Naval Forces, has decreed and made it a regulation that no other canines will be admitted as a member of the Royal Navy.

Yours faithfully,

Able Seaman J. Nuisance RN.

The other stereotyped letter, accepting the invitation in exactly the same manner as the above memorandum, but with the apologies deleted, stated the time at which the CO and Nuisance would arrive. It added that Nuisance would also be bringing a Leading Seaman Brown to act as his escort and ensure his good behaviour.

At the bottom of these letters was the personal signature of the CO, proving that not only had the senior naval officer approved (or deferred) these requests, but was the personal censor of all Nuisance's correspondence. Censorship was vital to security in the armed forces, but Nuisance was the only naval rating to have his mail signed by a commander. This was usually left to more junior naval officers.

Before any of these letters were posted the CO sent for Leading Seaman Brown to explain what was required of him. The CO interviewed Brown in private.

When Nuisance's escort appeared in the CO's office, he was shown a great pile of letters lying in a wire basket. The CO said: "Brown, these are the letters from people in the Peninsula requesting Nuisance's and my presence at charities in aid of the war effort. There are more than 60 letters in that basket and I have been able to accept only nine.

"When I do attend, Nuisance will accompany me, and you will be his escort. He will be on a leash at all times, in case any other animals are present. I don't want a dog-fight and a possible case of canine murder on my hands, understood?"

"Aye, aye sir," Brown replied.

"Tell me Brown, how is Nuisance getting along in your billet?"

The leading seaman could not restrain himself from relating to his CO the events concerning the little mongrel dog, and the parrot, aboard the ship in Cape Town docks. When he'd finished the CO was rolling about behind his desk with mirth and, taking a handkerchief from his pocket, wiped his eyes and said:

"Good God Brown, you and that dog have made my day. Wait until I tell that story to the rest of my officers in the wardroom tonight, they'll probably choke on their pink gins."

The leading seaman grinned.

"Well sir, the result is that there are two legends about Nuisance which have been proved untrue, one about him maiming or killing other dogs aboard ships in Cape Town, and another about him not being afraid of anything on two or four legs. That bird put the fear of the devil in him."

"Right Brown," continued the CO, "the MAA will give you plenty of notice about the dates when we are to attend these parties; just see that Nuisance has his cap in good order and his coat well-brushed. Dismissed".

The CO, Nuisance and the leading seaman over the next few weeks attended many of the events and Nuisance behaved himself impeccably. Nuisance was undoubtedly growing much wiser and familiar with ceremonies that were traditional customs of the Royal Navy.

Every time the Great Dane heard the notes of the national anthem God Save Our Gracious King, wherever he happened to be, the loyal AB would rise to his feet, tail swinging as if in time to the music. He would stand, black pug nose lifted slightly upwards, till the last verse was over — and then back to stand-easy.

Several times when Nuisance had been in Cape Town — having been granted week-end leave, that is a 48-hour pass — his oppos and civilians had watched him when the noon gun boomed over the town. Everyone then stood still to observe a two-minute silence in tribute to men of the allied forces at war. All moving vehicles also halted. Nuisance himself would assume a position of "at attention". If he saw anyone move during this two-minute silence he would bound across and place his great body in front of them, forcing the transgressor to a standstill.

Even if the offender was a naval rating, this was irrelevant to Nuisance and his confrontations, in view of his formidable size and menacing stance, would force them to heed the pause. When it was over and people or vehicles were on the move again, Nuisance would trot sedately away, tail swinging cheerfully, knowing that he had done his duty.

Many people in the Peninsula (possibly members of temperance societies or other bodies who deplored the drinking of alcoholic beverages) were convinced that Nuisance was a teetotaller. But any rating at *Afrikander*, and hundreds of servicemen who frequented hotels in Simon's Town and Cape Town and watched the canine AB downing three or four quarts of lager, could have shocked these well-intentioned people if they'd described the normal evening's intake by Nuisance.

One night Nuisance turned up at the Recreation Hall in Simon's Town in a condition known to most sailors as "three sheets in the wind."

The supervisor of this hall stated quite categorically to many ratings of *Afrikander* (several of whom were present and confirmed this) that Nuisance's four legs, instead of being in a north-to-south position, had a list to port and starboard of about 30 degrees from the vertical. There was an aura of lager fumes and his usually-bright brown eyes had a sort of grey film over them. He suddenly collapsed in a corner and three waitresses tried to revive him by pouring coffee down his gullet, but the liquid just trickled out again.

Hot tea was substituted, with the same result. Then one of the waitresses filled a tea-towel with ice-cubes and placed it on his head. Nuisance opened one eye, which had now assumed an opalescent hue; a snuffling noise sounded from his throat; he rubbed his eyes with one forepaw, and groaned. Patently he was suffering a king-size hangover.

The ice-cubes, however, must have had a beneficial effect. Five minutes later he raised his bleary eyes and lifting his head peered around the room. He rolled over on to his stomach, and was tempted by four meat pies which he sniffed speculatively, then gulped down.

He rose to his feet, a little shakily, stood quite straight, shook his head a couple of times as if to clear it, then held out his paw to the waitress who'd applied the ice-cubes on his head.

This girl had cured his hangover and the fact that she was a female, and not an oppo, made not the slightest difference. He felt like a new dog again, and wanted to show his appreciation.

Delightedly the samaritan shook the extended paw, and Nuisance walked in a straight line towards the door, pug nose uplifted, tail nearly vertical, sober as a judge, his gait full of haughty grandeur.

At the door he turned for one last glance at those present, as if to say, "everybody's entitled to a thrash now and again," opened his mouth as if to bark, thought better of the idea — and stalked out.

He was, of course, quite a Romeo when it came to enjoying the company of female Great Danes. Besides his 'wife' Judy, of the Prince Albert Hotel, Simon's Town, he had a second string to his bow, another of his breed named Adinda, of Hout Bay, who he had officially married on June 1, 1941.

According to his naval documents this made him a bigamist. It states clearly on his enlistment form that Judy was his wife and next-of-kin on August 25 1939. The bitch was still alive and no divorce had been granted. Ergo — he was a canine bigamist and living up to the reputation attributed to all his oppos about sailors having a girl in every port.

Some senior naval officers at *Afrikander* insist that Nuisance's marriage to Judy had been dissolved in late 1940. Whether this is true cannot be confirmed or denied; what is irrefutable is that Nuisance now had a new spouse, legal or not.

There is no doubt his oppos at *Afrikander* condoned, even approved, of him setting up a harem, if that was what Nuisance wanted. It was the dog's own choice and that was all that mattered — and sod anyone else.

The canine AB certainly did not appreciate or fail to display his contempt for human females, even young women in the Wrens, or Women's Royal Naval Service, even though on unofficial occasions some of the Wrens wore bell-bottomed trousers instead of skirts. But never with ratings' jumpers and blue collars, always primly retaining their fore-and-aft jackets.

If any female human attempted to force her attention on him, such as patting his head or stroking his back, Nuisance would shrug away and lope hastily off.

There are two incidents which give definite proof of this dislike. The CO of *Afrikander* had received several letters of complaint from Wrens and female citizens of the Peninsula regarding Nuisance's attitude towards them. However, in every letter there was a plea that they did not want the dog punished in any way.

There was a large ladies outfitters shop near the top of Adderley Street and Nuisance, on his many visits to Cape Town, used to lie stretched out right in front of the doorway of this emporium. Whenever a prospective female customer tried to enter the shop, the dog would rise and direct a menacing glare at the would-be buyer. In most cases the ladies would walk discreetly past.

This postcard, commemorating the "marriage" of the Great Danes Just Nuisance and Adinda at Hout Bay in June 1941, was sold in aid of the Naval Wartime Welfare Fund.

"ME AND MY GIRL"

A.B. "Just Nuisance," the "pal" of the Navy, was officially married to "ADINDA" on June 1st, 1941, at Hout Bay, C.P.

On a few occasions a naval rating would enter the establishment intent on buying something flimsy for his wife or girlfriend. Without hesitation Nuisance would enter the shop with one of these oppos, as if he wanted to help in some way. This gave some women an opportunity to enter the doorway no longer guarded by the Great Dane. If Nuisance noticed them opening the door he'd dart back and shove his head against it and close it once more, then rush to rejoin his oppo.

When the rating had bought what he wanted, Nuisance would follow him outside, extend his paw to be shaken, and resume his unauthorised guard duty. It was inevitable that some of these frustrated customers would finally report Nuisance to the CO.

The CO was left in a quandary.

In spite of the pleas for non-punishment of Nuisance, the CO believed he deserved some form of retribution, but was at a loss to decide under what section of Admiralty regulations he should be charged.

The canine AB was not drunk; he had not attacked anyone; nor was he on any premises forbidden to naval ratings. He was not obstructing pedestrians on the pavements, or vehicles in the road; nor had he uttered any audible threats (such as barking); nor was he loitering with intent; he had not displayed insolence towards, or refused to obey, the orders of a superior officer. In fact, after studying the Admiralty rules and regulations for half an hour, in despair he finally sent for Leading Seaman Brown, explained the position, pointed to the two large volumes of Admiralty rules, telling Brown that half an hour's study of them had not helped. He asked Nuisance's amanuensis if he had any solution.

Brown thought a moment then smiled:

"Yes sir, it's simple when you know Nuisance as well as I do. When a rating goes in the shop, Nuisance follows him in — is that right, sir?"

"That's so, according to some of these letters, Brown."

"Well sir, the answer is that whenever Nuisance is in town there are ratings from this base there as well. Simply post up a notice on all the news-boards in this base that any rating who sees Nuisance in this shop doorway, should coax him away."

Two weeks later the CO, after hearing that several ratings had enticed Nuisance away from the shop, was pleased and reassured.

The dog must have had some instinct that ratings didn't like to see him near the shop, and gave up his habit of lying in the entrance. As the years passed, however, there were occasions — though rare — when he did lie down in the very same door, but left after a few minutes instead of staying for several hours.

As a rule Nuisance's avoidance of all women was an automatic reflex, but there were exceptions. Like that time when the waitress cured his hangover, and Girlie Baker danced a waltz with him in the Mayor's Garden. Other than these two events the dog's temperament towards human females bordered on what the Royal Navy termed as "dumb insolence". (A rating smiling contemptuously at an officer, for instance, though not saying anything. Another case could be a rating who pretended he'd not heard a superior's order and, when asked to explain, refused to answer. There are variations too numerous to mention here.) But it accurately describes Nuisance's actions towards women better than any other I know of.

The other instance where Nuisance showed his contemptuous disregard for the ladies occurred at the City Hall in Cape Town, with disastrous but hilarious consequences.

This edifice held concerts for all servicemen and women. One evening a programme was billed and Nuisance, in the company of several oppos, entered the hall. He'd been there several times before and his adopted seat of honour was the middle of the aisle, level with the front row. In retrospect the word seat is incorrect; I should have said makeshift bed. Nuisance would lie down, pug nose facing the stage and the performers occupying it, and he had no compunctions about showing his annoyance if any act did not please him.

His great mouth would gape, followed by a loud yawn (heard above the music). Then he would emit a final encore, a loud whistling even mightier than his yawn.

When an act pleased him he would show his appreciation by raising his floppy ears, similar to a hunting dog scenting his prey, and when the act ended, would give one muted bark. Still several decibels too high for patrons seated nearby to enjoy, it drowned the applause of the other customers.

This particular evening a troupe of about eight dancing girls appeared on stage to perform a ballet routine. This was the first time Nuisance had seen an act with so many women in it. Three had been the most he'd ever encountered on the stage before. This was too much for him, so he rose quickly to all fours, leapt on the stage and started chasing the terrified girls round the raised platform.

There were a few of Nuisance's Simon's Town oppos in the hall and some of them clambered on the stage in an attempt to restrain the canine AB. Their motives were more concerned with trying to save Nuisance from getting into trouble, than acts of gallantry towards the girls. Pandemonium reigned for a while, with Nuisance, really entering into the fun, darting between the legs of his mates and bringing them crashing to the boards. The girls were screaming and scampering back and forth, the Great Dane blocking their attempts when they tried to flee back-stage.

One rating did manage to grab Nuisance's collar, but a jerk of that giant head sent him flying. Nuisance was enjoying the melee with a spirit of abandon that was awe-inspiring. He barked continuously, the noise reverberating round the hall and echoing up Adderley Street.

Luckily a naval patrol of six ratings in charge of a petty officer made for the building at the double. They all wore white gaiters and belts and arm bands with the letters NP emblazoned on them. Each of the ratings was armed with a truncheon or belaying pin, as naval personnel called it.

As this rescue party entered the majority of the audience were streaming through the exit, either in panic or chuckling with amusement. The NP squad approached the stage platform where four of Nuisance's oppos had managed to calm him down, allowing the girls to reach safety. The petty officer, who already knew of Nuisance from previous demonstrations in town, asked one of the dog's oppos, who happened to be a killick, what all the commotion was about. They had better have a good explanation or he was going to arrest the lot, including Nuisance.

The killick was intelligent and a fast thinker. He told the enraged PO that Nuisance had seen a large rat running across the stage and pursued it. It was bad luck that this happened just as eight girls were about to begin their dance act. If there'd been fewer of them undoubtedly Nuisance would have caught the rodent. The other three seamen backed the killick's story. It was plain from the expression on the PO's face that he didn't believe them, but he sighed and waved away his henchmen. The battle area was now quiet, with Nuisance and his four oppos the heroic victors.

The matter didn't end there. The next day there was a notice pinned on the City Hall's billboard, signed by the manager, that as from this day Nuisance was barred from admission.

This ruling raised such an outcry from both ratings and citizens of Cape Town, plus a memo from the CO of *Afrikander* to management, that the note was torn down. A new rule stated that Able Seaman Nuisance was welcome to every comfort and facility the City Hall could provide.

This finally confirmed the admiration, respect and affection, amounting almost to reverence, in which Nuisance was held by all servicemen and women, civilians too, living in the Cape Peninsula.

On September 9, 1941, the CO of *HMS Afrikander I* issued a memo to all canteens, service institutes and main hotels in Simon's Town and Cape Town. It read:

The Commanding Officer of *H M S Afrikander I*, Simon's Town, CP, respectfully asks that the heads of all services canteens, institutes, etc, and managers of hotels in Simon's Town, Cape Town, and their suburbs co-operate in controlling the canine rating known as Able Seaman Nuisance from partaking of excessive amounts of alcoholic drinks in their establishments. I am not suggesting that this rating should not be served alcoholic beverages, only that the quantity be restricted. My Regulating Staff in the Guardroom have reported that on several occasions during the past few months he has passed through that Guardroom, requiring the assistance of other ratings to maintain his balance due to being drunk.

After making enquiries I have ascertained that this over-indulgence is the result of ratings from this base buying him drinks and all personnel stationed here have been warned of the consequences if they persist in their generosity to such an extent that this rating is inebriated.

I would therefore be obliged if when you see that this Able Seaman has

consumed his allowed amount of lager for the night (about six quarts) without becoming drunk, you will please inform the ratings in his company that he is not permitted to drink further amounts. Should any rating refuse your request you have my permission to call the nearest NP (whose .telephone numbers are known to you all) and they will enforce my orders.
Thank you for your co-operation,
Sgd, Commanding Officer,
HMS Afrikander I,
Simon's Town.

Ex-Chief Petty Officer Brown still has a copy in his possession of this memo, but it is in such a poor condition I was not able to obtain a copy clear enough to include in this book. He admits that he stole it from the notice-board of the NAAFI canteen at Simon's Town the day after it was· first displayed.

The recipients of these memos pinned them up and it seems that the guardroom regulating staff confirmed that this warning was heeded by all ratings at *Afrikander*. After all, if Nuisance was placed on a charge for being drunk he would lose his Nutty (milk chocolate bars) ration, several bottles of lager which were allowed at cheap rates and suffer banishment from the NAAFI (Navy, Army, Air Force Institutes) for a month. This would have left the AB chocker as he loved to have a drink with his oppos in this club, especially during the lunch-time stand-easy period.

One night soon after this, approaching Christmas of 1941, Nuisance chummed up with an acting petty officer. This was not surprising as an APO wore square-rig for 12 months before his rank was confirmed. He then had to change into fore-and-aft rig. He wore more crossed anchors on his upper sleeve than a rating, the anchors surmounted by a royal crown.

After swigging down a large quantity of lager in celebration of his promotion from leading seaman, which had happened only that morning, he was quite tiddly. So Nuisance — as was his custom when any of his oppos were staggering under the influence — took the acting PO's sleeve in his strong jaws and helped him towards the Simon's Town Sailors and Soldiers Home. Nuisance always had a bed reserved for him at this hostel, as he had at the Union Jack Club in Cape Town. But that night the official in charge led the PO to the chiefs' and petty officers' dormitory, which was separate from the room which ratings occupied.

The official was new to the job, though he had been informed about the Great Dane's privilege of a reserved bed in the ratings' quarters. Having let the PO into the PO's dormitory, the official went back to his desk.

Nuisance decided he should see his new-found oppo to bed, so went in the room with him. Several chiefs and PO's were either already asleep or getting ready for bed. A couple of them coming to the PO's assistance, undressed him and laid him out in a bed where, within a few seconds, he was fast asleep. Nuisance, faithful to his own kind, and seeing a bed vacant next to his oppo, jumped into that. One of the chiefs removed the dog's cap and placed it at the foot of the bunk. Several of the other PO's who were still awake laughed at this blatant infringement of naval regulations, but were happy enough to have this canine AB as a visitor staying over-night.

A problem arose when another petty officer entered the room and saw every bed occupied.

He turned and left, intending to find another bed at some other hostel. But as he passed the official this man asked why he was leaving after having paid for a bed. The PO answered that the dormitory was full. The official looked at his log-book and insisted there was a bed vacant, got up and walked to the PO's dormitory. His face darkened in a scowl when he saw Nuisance in a bed.

The official was quite a tall man and broad, in early middle age, and told the PO he'd soon put the animal in its rightful place. He moved towards Nuisance and placed his hand on the dog's collar. The AB had just about dropped off to sleep. He growled in warning and the official, looking at the long canine teeth, lost some of his confidence and moved away.

He then went into the ratings' dormitory and asked three of them if they'd help to shift Nuisance. After all, he belonged with them, not PO's and often there was little love lost between ratings and petty officers, either on duty or on shore leave.

The four of them approached Nuisance, who was half asleep. The night supervisor got hold of the collar and gave it a sharp tug, lifting the dog's head off the pillow, and tried to pull the hound out of bed.

Nuisance, usually docile towards human beings, had a limit to his patience, and it had been passed.

A loud snarl, and he sprang out of bed. The three ratings stepped back in alarm as the dog launched his muscled body at the official, and when he struck it was his two front paws that hit his tormentor on the chest, much the same thing as a human being shoving with outstretched arms at an opponent.

The official's breath left his lungs with a loud shoosh! The force knocked him backwards and over one of the bunks in which a petty officer lay. Then the victim's head hit the wall and he lay dazed on the floor.

Nuisance advanced again and everyone thought the dog was going for the man's unprotected throat — but the Great Dane just sniffed at the man's head, then walked back to his bunk.

The three ratings went up to Nuisance, who held out his paw for a handshake. One of the seamen tied on the dog's cap and he left the room with his tail swinging smartly from side to side, always an indication that he had regained his normally quiet temperament. The ratings took him to the bed reserved for him in their dormitory, untied his cap, tucked him in bed for the second time and, in a few minutes, Nuisance was fast asleep.

In the morning the three ratings accompanied Nuisance back to his billet in *Afrikander* and explained all that had happened to Leading Seaman

Brown. (He still has an excellent memory of the incident, as related to him by a rating, and can also recall going up to the dog and telling him that he was "in the rattle" — otherwise due to be charged with an offence against naval regulations — properly this time.)

Apparently Nuisance thought Brown was scolding him for something he'd done wrong and held out his forepaw and Brown, with a grin, shook hands. The official recovered quickly and wrote a letter about it to *Afrikander*'s CO. Being a fair-minded man, he did state in his letter that although the dog had infringed rules, the attack on him was in self-defence. This was the second letter of complaint in three days. The first had come from a ticket collector who had found Nuisance travelling to Cape Town without his season ticket. The copper wire which his escort had threaded through the cardboard and twisted to the collar ring had cut through the cardboard. In fact a dockyard worker had found the card the same evening that Nuisance had lost it, lying in the road, and handed it in to the guardroom. The staff had re-fastened it to Nuisance's collar when he returned next morning.

This ticket-collector craftily noted that he had not reported the absence of Nuisance's ticket to his superior as he didn't want to get the dog in trouble, but according to regulations Nuisance *had* committed an offence.

The CO had showed the letter to Leading Seaman Brown, who muttered that all ticket collectors on the Simon's Town to Cape Town trains knew the dog had a season ticket.

The CO assured Brown that when Nuisance appeared before him on two charges he would take the final case of travelling on the SAR without a ticket as being a technical offence; he would award the least possible punishment for this offence. He also asked Brown to trace any chiefs or PO's who had been in the PO's dormitory the night Nuisance had intruded there.

The CO told Brown there would be two separate charges regarding this event, plus the ticket charge — three charges altogether to be answered in one day. The CO couldn't say how they would be worded — that was the master-at-arms' prerogative, but Brown was to escort Nuisance to the MAA's office in three days when the captain of *Afrikander* adjudicated at his weekly meeting of requestmen and defaulters. (Requestmen were PO's and ratings asking for promotion, long leave, or special privileges; defaulters appeared last, these all facing a charge or charges under Admiralty rules and regulations.)

"Off Caps"

At nine o'clock one Monday morning just before Christmas 1941, Leading Seaman Brown led Nuisance into the master-at-arms' office in the admin block at *HMS Afrikander I*. Inside the office was the MAA and his chief assistant, the regulating petty officer.

The senior warrant officer looked at Brown:

"The CO wants you to escort Nuisance when he appears before him and, as this able seaman cannot speak in his own defence, are you willing to act as his spokesman?"

"Aye, aye Master," replied Brown, and was told to wait in the corridor alongside five other ratings who were defaulters.

Nuisance's oppos in the billet had worked hard that morning getting him ready to appear before the CO. After breakfast they had given the dog a good shower, dried him off, brushed him down, added a little brilliantine to the brush, so the tawny coat fairly gleamed. They had bought a new hat and cap tally with the letters HMS emblazoned in gold coloured thread on the ribbon, as his old one was getting a bit battered, with a sagging brim.

It was tied on his head between his ears and was completely horizontal,

(a rating who wore his hat flat-a-back, tilted on the back of his head or pushed over one ear, could be charged with being incorrectly dressed.)

Usually, all defaulters entered the CO's office in strict alphabetical order, but the MAA opened the door, stuck his head out in the corridor and shouted:

"Able Seaman Nuisance and escort, the CO has decided to deal with you first. Step into the office. Smartly, left, right, left, right . . . ."

Brown took Nuisance into the office where the CO sat behind his desk. Alongside him was his number 1 or second-in-command, and the MAA stood at the other side. The CO had Nuisance's service documents laid open on his desk top. The MAA looked at the clipboard sheet in his hand to which were fixed the charge sheets and opened the proceedings.

"Able Seaman Nuisance you appear before your commanding officer charged with three offences. It has been decided that Leading Seaman Brown will speak on your behalf.

"The first charge is that, prejudicial to naval discipline, you did travel on a train while not having a ticket for that journey. Guilty or not guilty?"

Brown answered:

"Guilty sir, but the Able Seaman pleads extenuating circumstances."

The leading seaman had been well-coached by a lieutenant who had been a lawyer in civil life and was anxious to help Nuisance.

The MAA intoned the next charge . . .

"That the accused did appropriate a bed in the petty officers' dormitory at the Sailors' and Soldiers' Home, Simon's Town, to which his rank of able seaman did not entitle him. Guilty or not guilty?"

Brown replied:

"Guilty, sir, but again with extenuating circumstances. Three petty officers of this base who were present have written affidavits of their evidence on behalf of this rating, sir, which I believe are attached to this able seaman's documents."

The CO nodded and the MAA continued . . .

"That Able Seaman Nuisance did resist ejection from the above-named dormitory. Guilty or not guilty?"

Brown answered.

"Guilty sir, but only in self-defence to an attack made on him by the night supervisor of the hostel. The three petty officers' affidavits also contain evidence to support this."

Nuisance, again bored with his surroundings, tried to sit down, his mouth open in a wide yawn. All three prosecution officers stifled grins. Brown lifted the dog to all fours but, in doing so, Nuisance's head caught the front of the desk and knocked his cap askew. Brown straightened the cap and the CO, looking at the MAA, commented:

"Master, I regret to inform you that the order 'Off Caps' was not given by you before the charges were read out; please do so now."

The MAA looked flustered for a moment, then gave the order.

Brown untied the chin strap of Nuisance's cap, removed it and stood with it in his hand. Meanwhile the CO was scanning the affidavits made by the petty officers in Nuisance's defence. Then he spoke.

"On the first charge Able Seaman Nuisance you are guilty beyond all doubt. The regulating staff here confirm that your free pass was handed in to the guardroom and obviously you were not wearing it on the train. However it is beyond doubt that you were unaware of this, therefore your punishment is that you be confined to the banks of Lily Pond at Froggy Pond, all lamp-posts removed. This punishment is suspended indefinitely unless you incur a similar charge in the near future.

"On the second charge, of sleeping in an unauthorised place, you are also found guilty, but it is a fact that another petty officer accompanied you into that room and, being drunk, was not aware of the possible consequences and it is due to your concern for his safety that you were in that room. Punishment is that you are deprived of bones for seven days. This punishment is also suspended due to extenuating circumstances.

"On the third charge I find you not guilty. I will not condone or allow any man under my command to be victimised or attacked. That this happened is borne out by the affidavits of petty officers who witnessed this assault on your person. Charge dismissed.

"Master-at-arms, the punishments and charges will be entered on this rating's conduct sheet, but no reference made to the suspension of those charges. That is all. Leading Seaman Brown, will you please escort the rating out of this office and leave him with one of the other ratings outside?

"I wish to discuss something with you, so please return promptly."

Brown eyed his CO apprehensively, but fastened on Nuisance's cap, led him outside and asked one of the defaulters to look after him. He re-entered the office and stiffened to attention in front of his commander.

The CO looked up and murmured:

"Stand easy, Leading Seaman Brown. This discussion is both unofficial and confidential, understood?"

"Aye, aye sir," replied Brown.

"It has been brought to my attention during the past few months that Able Seaman Nuisance has suffered a certain amount of discomfort and has had to be assisted by his shipmates in removing and putting on his cap. Does this rating seem pleased to be wearing this cap, or not?"

"Well sir," answered Brown, "to be honest, Nuisance doesn't exactly object to wearing the cap, but he does shift his head round a bit when we put it on, as if he doesn't find it comfortable. And when we take it off at night, I know it sounds funny sir, but he gives a sort of sigh of relief, if you take my meaning sir."

"Very well Brown, I think you've made your point. In strict confidence, I am going to ask the C-in-C South Atlantic if this rating can be excused from wearing a cap, except on full ceremonial parades.

"This is setting a second precedent in the Royal Navy for any rating or officer. Firstly, he is the only animal to be granted official status as a member of the Royal Navy, and I rather think the C-in-C himself hasn't the necessary authority to grant this request and will have to refer the matter to the Admiralty in London by radio communication. But I'm sure that, if the admiral recommends this action to Naval HQ at home, they will agree.

"That is all Brown, and keep this to yourself."

Brown left the office with elation. Nuisance had escaped all actual punishment and it was possible that soon the dog would be able to walk about unencumbered by headgear.

When all the ratings heard the CO's decisions regarding the charges, those in Nuisance's room cheered, then wished they hadn't when Nuisance lifted his head and barked just once, the ratings swearing on oath that the sound rattled all the room's windows and, if the door hadn't been open, would have cracked them as well.

A week later a memo was pinned to all notice boards in the base that the C-in-C South Atlantic had authorised Able Seaman J. Nuisance, *HMS Afrikander I,* to be excused from wearing a naval cap.

At the end of the year 1941, Leading Seaman Brown was drafted to a destroyer that called at Simon's Town, as a replacement for one of its crew who had appendicitis and had been brought ashore to Simon's Town Naval Hospital.

The drafting officer had a word with *Afrikander*'s CO who suggested that Leading Seaman Clark from Froggy Pond, who had been Nuisance's escort, should be Brown's replacement at *Afrikander*.

Clark arrived that afternoon carrying his kit-bag and hammock and Brown was just about ready to leave the room. The two killicks knew each other well and Brown filled in his oppo on Nuisance's recent experiences – especially about the dog being given permission not to wear a hat.

As the two killicks went out they met Nuisance returning for a kip. Brown dropped his hammock and kit-bag, hugged the Great Dane and shook his paw in farewell, while Clark shook it in greeting. The dog looked curiously at both of them and then trotted off for his snooze . . . .

At the end of each year the CO, in conjunction with an officer of the writer branch, filled in a report on the service documents of officers, chiefs, petty officers and ratings under his command, assisted by reports from officers in charge of non-commissioned personnel. The CO, assisted by his second-in-command, made his own personal assessment of officers.

As they sat in the CO's office the lieutenant writer came to Nuisance's conduct sheet, and asked his CO what he should put down. The CO looked at the three charges listed on the sheet, and punishments for these offences, and told the writer to inscribe the following.

Character — Very good. Efficiency — Moderate. Discipline — Poor. *(These descriptions can be seen on copies of Nuisance's conduct sheets in Simon's Town Museum, and the British Imperial War Museum, London.)*

There were many rumours about Nuisance's preferences for food and drink, even among ratings, at Froggy Pond and *Afrikander*. The facts are these. Nuisance was a strict meat-and-bone man, and for "afters" he favoured puddings spread with custard or vanilla ice-cream.

One kind of meat he could not abide.

Once the chief cook at *Afrikander* had laid out a plateful of pigs' trotters (a great favourite and rare meal for ratings), but Nuisance sniffed at them disdainfully and promptly turned the plate over with his paw. Resignedly the chief cook sliced roast pork from a large haunch, and laid these on the floor. Nuisance repeated his previous act of rejection. Finally, as no more cooked meat was available, he fed the dog with a couple of large tins filled with corned beef.

Nuisance gulped these down with pleasure, and held out both paws, begging for a second helping . . .

The chief cook, in spite of his chief petty officer's rank, was the dog's slave and fed this starving canine with another helping of corned beef, washed down with a quart of creamy milk.

Nuisance loved milk chocolate and ice-cream; caramels he'd accept, but then get a bit stroppy when they got stuck in his great molars. He'd approach a rating, shove his pug nose at him and open up his huge jaws, trying to masticate this sweet-tasting but aggravating toffee, until the oppo reached in his mouth and removed the gunge.

Boiled sweets he'd suck for a few moments and spit out. If he snatched at a strong mint without smelling it first, he'd flip it from his jaws with his lolloping tongue, kick the mint away with one foot and glare at the rating who'd given it him, as if to say, "I shan't forget that, mate".

Fruit, vegetables and bread were anathema to him, though he did like certain types of pastry that contained cream or chocolate.

Lager was his favourite tipple. At least it was till I introduced him to another type of tipple, when I first met him in November 1942. Water was to be drunk only as a last resort when his huge body was suffering from acute dehydration. His oppos were so generous with gifts of lager, that he'd probably forgotten what water tasted like. Milk was his next favourite drink to beer, but not canned milk, which he would ignore.

After his rejection of pig meat the chief cook always swore that he had a touch of the Muslim religion and believed that he would never enter paradise if he ate it.

Such were Nuisance's likes and dislikes regarding food and drink.

One day in the early months of 1924, a British County Class cruiser entered Table Bay and anchored. Usually large warships proceeded to Simon's Town, where they could take stores, or have a major overhaul if they required repairs. Whatever the reason for this visit is really irrelevant, except that its presence eventually spelled trouble for Nuisance.

The cruiser was in the bay for five days and during that time some of the ship's crew, especially the ratings, became friendly with the RN's Great Dane. By now, of course, Nuisance had become a legend throughout most ships of the Navy, and even in some shore bases in the UK.

On the night before the cruiser was to weigh anchor in the morning, to proceed on her voyage, some of the ship's crew smuggled Nuisance aboard the pinnace which ferried them back to their ship. How they got the huge dog past the deck officer on watch at the top of the cruiser's gangway is not clear, but perhaps one of the returning party engaged the officer in conversation while his oppos slipped Nuisance past.

The ratings hid the dog, probably in one of the mess decks. Some petty officers must have connived at the abduction as part of their duties consisted of inspecting all ratings' mess-decks every few hours. Like Lord Nelson, they must have turned a blind eye to Nuisance's presence; he was too large to be hidden in any small nook in the mess accessible to ratings.

The cruiser sailed at 11 the next morning and was three miles out when Nuisance escaped his kidnappers, shot up the steps of a hatchway, saw the huge mass of Table Mountain receding in the distance and leapt overboard.

He started swimming strongly towards shore, but the sea at this point was curling with short waves and there was a strong cross-current. But the physical strength of Nuisance was such that he kept swimming strongly for shore. It was learnt afterwards that the Port Captain in Cape Town Docks had been watching the cruiser's departure from his office through a telescope and actually saw Nuisance jump into the sea. He nearly ordered a launch out to pick up the dog, but was convinced that Nuisance would make shore without help. He kept his telescope trained on the dog and determined to have a boat out if Nuisance showed signs that the sea and tide were overwhelming him.

Nuisance succeeded in his swim ashore without help but, when he reached the pier, was exhausted.

The Port Captain, with two of his staff, helped the tired canine AB to his office, wrapped him in a blanket and rubbed the dog dry with a towel. He then poured a small quantity of brandy down Nuisance's throat, but this didn't seem to help much, and the Great Dane lay stretched out on his side, his great chest heaving with rasping breaths and his eyes bloodshot from salt-water.

The Port Captain phoned the CO at *Afrikander I* who at once arranged for a thirty-hundredweight truck, driven by his own driver, to fetch the dog back to the base at Simon's Town.

When the lorry arrived back at *Afrikander* carrying the press-ganged AB, the CO was waiting at the guardroom and, after taking one look at the dog who was still lying on his side on the floor of the vehicle, immediately ordered Nuisance to be driven to the sick-bay.

The surgeon-commander had Nuisance laid on a stretcher and carried to the examination room.

After a medical check which lasted half an hour the base's senior doctor diagnosed that Nuisance was suffering from extreme exhaustion and would have to spend 48 hours in bed at the hospital. He would be given potions to help him regain his strength. To ensure complete silence (as the MO said the best cure of all would be plenty of rest and sleep) Nuisance was placed in a cot in the isolation ward. There were four beds, but he was the only patient.

The MO informed the CO that his canine patient was to receive plenty of glucose drinks and vitamin tablets, but the dog's magnificent physical constitution would allow him a better chance of recovery than if he'd been human.

He saw Nuisance tucked safely in his hospital cot and, with the aid of a male nurse, managed to pour a dose of medicine down the dog's throat though the canine patient growled at this ill-treatment. However, he then laid his head on the pillow, gave a massive yawn and went straight to sleep.

The sick-bay's male nurses looked in on Nuisance from time to time during the afternoon, but the dog slept on.

Late that afternoon the CO sent for Leading Seaman Clark to inform him of events. The big leading seaman muttered softly that if the same cruiser docked in Table Bay again, its crew had better remain on board and not enter Cape Town or they'd be "filled in" by ratings from *Afrikander* for having shanghaied their oppo.

The CO smiled and promised that if that happened he'd have a personal word with the cruiser's captain.

Still muttering dire threats of revenge, the killick left the CO's office and went to the sick-bay to visit Nuisance, but the MO in charge turned him away. Nuisance was allowed no visitors till late the next day.

Leading Seaman Clark returned to his billet and passed on to the ratings the facts the CO had given him. Above all, Nuisance would be fit as ever in the next couple of days, and this cheered up all the dog's oppos.

About eight that evening one of the sick-bay attendant's making his rounds, heard the sound of scraping coming from the closed door of the isolation ward, followed by two thunderous barks which must have woken every patient in the hospital.

The attendant hurried to the door and opened it, and found Nuisance sitting by the door holding his paw out for a handshake. The bed Nuisance had been recuperating in looked as if a typhoon had raged over it – the pillow, sheets, blankets and mattress strewn all round the floor.

The cot itself had been moved a couple of metres from its original position and was jammed tight up against the next bed – no mean task this would have been for a couple of the attendants, as the legs of the cots had no castors.

The attendant gathered up the mattress, sheets, blankets and pillow then placed them on the cot, re-making the bed; but in spite of all attempts to coax the dog back into bed, he had to give up in disgust.

The medical orderly pressed a bell-push and the duty MO arrived, a lieutenant not the senior MO who had ordered Nuisance into the bed that afternoon.

The attendant explained to the doctor what had happened and that his patient would not get back into the cot. The MO took Nuisance's medical chart from the bedrail and scanned what his senior surgeon had written

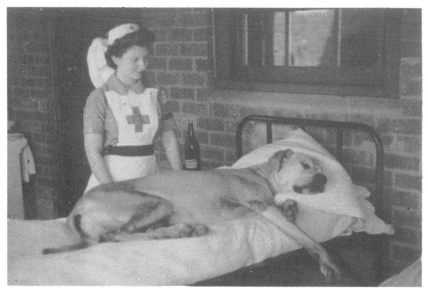

Just Nuisance as a patient in the naval hospital, Simon's Town, in September 1943. Note the quart bottle of "medicinal" Lion Special, on the bedside table.

when Nuisance was admitted.

He cautiously approached the new patient, who was now sitting on his haunches, paws dangling from his front legs in a begging position. The doctor placed a stethoscope to Nuisance's muscled chest and listened intently to the heart-beat and breathing. He removed the instrument then, taking one of the dog's forepaws, tested Nuisance's nervous reflexes, but this fuss was too much for Nuisance who started growling. The MO backed sharply away from his patient, proving that at least the doctor's nervous reflexes were ticking over smartly.

Gathering courage, the medic opened Nuisance's great jaws, shone a pencil-beam torch down the throat, then in each of Nuisance's eyes, and backed away in a hurry as the dog growled again. He shook his head in bewilderment and, remarking that the dog was perfectly fit again, scrawled acros the medical chart: "Patient discharged, fit to resume duty."

The MO asked the attendant if he knew Nuisance's billet and ordered him to take the ex-patient there.

On opening the hut door all the ratings and Leading Seaman Clark greeted their restored oppo with cheers.

(When I interviewed ex-Chief Petty Officer Clark he remembered the event and descriptions as if, in his own words, "it was like it happened only yesterday".)

The whole base had heard about Nuisance's latest adventure and throughout the afternoon and evening there had been countless enquiries at the hospital as to the canine AB's progress – by officers, chiefs, petty officers and ratings.

As the male nurse was leaving, Leading Seaman Clark asked, "Has Nuisance had any grub since he left the harbour?"

The sick-bay attendant eyed the killick's big frame and replied, "Not a scrap, but don't blame me mate, it was the surgeon-commander's orders when Nuisance was admitted to hospital."

"Well sometimes these butchers have no idea what's good for a bloke, or a dog either," replied the killick.

The leading seaman patted down Nuisance's bed and spoke to the dog, who sat listening to an oppo playing a mouth organ. The hound loved the sound of a "fluitjie" – providing the performer didn't repeat the tune of the British national anthem too many times, as he had to stand at attention every time *that* was played.

"Come on Nuisance, have a bit of a kip, then I'll take you to the galley." At the word "galley", Nuisance's ears pricked, he knew what this meant, and headed straight for the door.

The killick laughed, reached for his cap, and followed Nuisance, saying, "Come on then gannet. I expect you've had enough sleep this afternoon – it's big eats you want, isn't it old lad?" He opened the door and left, with Nuisance trotting expectantly several yards ahead of him, then looking back as if urging the killick to get a move on.

The PO cook lit a big stove range, reached down a huge frying pan from a hook, put a load of fat in it, went to the fridge and came out with an armful of lamb chops.

Nuisance was prowling round the stove, jaws slavering in anticipation, his black damp pug nose lifting upwards to savour the aroma of the cooking meat. The big head appeared above the range top so he could catch sight of his meal, jaws dribbling.

Clark pulled him down both times. "Take it easy, you bloody old gannet; won't be long before that stomach of yours is full again."

The cook set out the steaming chops on a tin beer tray – and there must have been a dozen or so succulent offerings of meat before him. Eagerly he gave his first lick but it was still so hot that it burnt his tongue. He let out a whimpering howl of frustration and pain, then for the next few minutes circled the meal, mouth gaping, ears upright and tail wagging frantically.

Finally the starving AB could stand the suspense no longer. He lifted his right paw, licked it clean, and placed it on one of the chops. Satisfied that they were now cool enough to eat, he dug into his "big eats".

Not forgetting table manners, however. Each chop was picked up separately, masticated and swallowed. An average of about 15 seconds for each thick slice of lamb.

When he'd disposed of every last scrap, he sat down in a begging position, asking for more. Clark and the cook looked at each other, both grinning.

The cook laid out a saucepan of fresh milk. Nuisance soon lapped that up and trotted over and held out his paw in a gesture of gratitude – even though the cook wore fore-and-aft rig. Incidents like this again disprove the theory that exists to this day that Nuisance ignored any naval personnel unless they were ratings. If any one showed unusual acts of kindness towards him the Great Dane would show his gratitude in some way.

That night a tired-out Nuisance slept soundly, and when the Tannoy system blared out "wakey-wakey" early the next morning the dog was still drowsy. Instead of leaping out of bed as usual, he lifted his head off the pillow, yawned, and lay down again.

Then he saw the rest of his oppos disappearing out of the door and knew they were bound for the dining hall and breakfast. A dog, even after a late supper, needed to keep up his strength, so he bounded after them, licking Clark's hand as he passed the killick.

A couple of days later Clark noticed that Nuisance was limping and unable to run. At first he thought nothing of it but, as the days passed, the limp grew worse. Even lying in bed the dog was constantly licking his front right paw.

Clark examined the pads, thinking Nuisance might have a thorn or a sliver of glass imbedded. There was nothing to see, even though he used a magnifying glass loaned to him by an oppo. Then he pressed the bone, thinking that Nuisance would show some sign of pain, but there was no reaction. Then he examined the upper leg without results.

The killick that afternoon took Nuisance, now limping badly, to the MAA's office, and asked if he could take the dog to the sick-bay for an X-ray. The MAA called for a small van and told Clark to let him know what was wrong. He would report to the CO.

A petty officer male nurse at the reception desk made out a medical card for the canine patient, then disappeared down a corridor, returning a few minutes later saying that the senior medical officer, a surgeon-commander, would examine the patient.

He led Clark and Nuisance into a large room full of gleaming surgical equipment. The SMO was seated behind his desk wearing a medical smock and watched Nuisance intently as he limped in.

He gestured for Clark to put Nuisance on the examining couch. which the killick managed to do with difficulty in spite of his strength. Clark reported that several times before Nuisance had shown signs of a slight limp, but it had always disappeared.

The surgeon-commander rolled Nuisance on his side and, starting at the top of the right front leg worked his way down prodding and pushing at bones and muscles. Then he held up the right forepaw, took one keen look at it and laughed, asking if the killick had really examined it. The killick replied that he had, even using a magnifying glass. The SMO chuckled at the puzzled expression on his face, as he asked if Nuisance would require an operation.

The SMO answered:

"Of course he will, leading seaman, but what amuses me is the fact that you examined Nuisance's foot with a magnifying glass and couldn't find the trouble. A man who is half-blind could have told you."

"Will it be a big operation sir, and will he be able to run about like he could before?" asked Clark.

The commander grinned again and replied:

"The operation will take about one minute, no anaesthetic required, and Nuisance won't feel a thing. In another minute he'll be running about fast as ever, faster probably."

Clark was astounded.

"If there is something in one of his pads, sir, how come I missed it?"

"Ever heard of an ingrowing toenail, Clark?

"Come over here, hold out the dog's right paw please, and keep the limb still while I use a pair of incisors. We'll have this rating right in no time at all.

"Luckily the in-growing claw, or nail as we would call it, hasn't yet penetrated the tender skin, but in another day or two would have. Every time Nuisance puts his weight on the paw, however, this nail pushes into the skin – see it, Clark?"

The killick wondered how he'd missed it. One of the claws had doubled round on itself.

The surgeon gave one snip and a part of the claw, nearly 20 mm long and crescent-shaped, flipped to the floor.

Clark let go Nuisance's paw and picked up the horny nail, asking the SMO if he could keep it.

When Nuisance stood on the floor, he took a tentative step obviously expecting pain. But, discovering there was none, he began to prance around the examination room in ecstasy. Lifting up that black pug nose, he gave out a rollicking obbligato of grateful barks.

The SMO clapped his hands over his ears and yelled to get the dog out. Clark, forgetting the surgeon's rank, shook his hand, mumbled apologies and with a broad grin of relief on his face opened the door.

Nuisance took off down the corridor like a greyhound, nearly knocking over patients and sick-bay attendants who had stepped out of their rooms in response to Nuisance's lion-like rendition of pleasure and freedom from pain.

The dog shot out of the building and made off into the distance, not re-appearing again in the billet for a couple of hours where Clark was proudly displaying the keepsake claw.

After this episode, another of the rumours about Nuisance was disproved. The one concerning the dog's rejection of officers. Whenever the hound was anywhere near the SMO he'd approach the surgeon and hold out the paw for a handshake. The doctor always responded . . . .

Ex-Chief Petty Officer Clark still has this piece of claw in a small leather wallet. When I told him it would fetch quite a sum if sent to the Cape and auctioned off, he shook his grizzled head and replied, "Not for all the tea in China; that bit of Nuisance is going to be buried with me when I hit the deep six."

I hope this will not happen for many years . . . .

Another habit Nuisance developed happened by accident. Usually when the last train from Cape Town arrived at Simon's Town, Nuisance was the first to alight. One night, however, he dropped off to sleep on the train, as he'd been on a light 'thrash', and woke up to find the ticket-collector trying to wake up those ratings still in their seats, drunk or nearly so.

Nuisance went from compartment to compartment helping the railway conductor to wake his oppos. The dog would grip the cuffs of their sleeves between his jaws and pull them to the floor. This woke most of them up, but others were too far gone in alcoholic dreamland. They just groaned and went back to sleep.

The canine AB then bounded out to the platform, and caught up with the ratings near the station exit. Catching one by the cuff, he dragged him back to the carriages.

When the rating saw his mates lying on the carriage floors he yelled for his pals to help him. A dozen or more ran back to the coaches and helped the dozey sailors to stand, then led them down the platform to the exit.

They managed to get them sober enough to walk through the guardroom gate, Nuisance insisting on guiding one half-slewed oppo by his arm.

After this episode, Nuisance repeated his performance every time he caught the last train from Cape Town – and there weren't many nights that he didn't save some of his fellow seamen from being adrift.

His intelligence was such that he repeated the performance at Cape Town station with drowsy matelots. One sharp tug and they'd wake up, startled to find themselves at journey's end.

The ticket-collectors were delighted with his help as, drunk or sober, no seaman likes being woken up from a kip. If they saw it was Nuisance who'd roused them, however, they'd accept it with a smile and a pat of the dog's great head. If it was a ticket-collector, ratings could get quite stroppy. There was no-one more amiable and friendly than Royal Navy men, as many people in the Cape can testify. But Jack Tar was a tough customer indeed when upset for some reason, and many a ticket-collector had received a bloody nose or a couple of teeth knocked out when trying to help their assailants.

In mid-1942, Nuisance was knocked over by a car in one of Cape Town's suburbs, but managed to make his way back to *Afrikander* without help. He was put in sick-bay for two days, X-rayed, proving no bones were broken, but he had several bruises round his shoulders.

Cold compresses were used and the SMO ensured that the dog stayed in bed for two whole days by having ratings in attendance, replaced every four hours. By also having the chief cook feed him and bring him plenty of milk to drink, this victim of a hit-and-run driver was kept immobile.

On his third day in hospital the SMO, with Leading Seaman Clark in company, visited Nuisance. As I have stated, whenever the SMO came within range the dog never forgot who'd cured him of his lameness and would hold out his paw to be shaken.

The surgeon-commander removed the wrappings from the bruised Nuisance and all swellings had vanished. The doctor turned to Clark and said: "Alright Leading Seaman Clark, Nuisance can go back to his own billet; that dog's got the constitution of an ox. You may be a fine figure of a man Clark, but it would have taken a week for you to recover from the injuries this animal suffered."

Clark grinned at the Senior MO and replied:

"I know that sir, if this dog could box he'd be the heavyweight champion of the Cape Peninsula Naval Force, not me."

The dog cheerfully followed Clark down the sick-bay corridor without showing discomfort and, once outside, broke into a run watched affectionately by the big seaman.

A few days after this Clark was sent for by his CO and informed that the Senior Naval Officer had accepted an invitation for himself and Nuisance to attend a charity affair which was to take place at the house and garden of a lady resident in Green Point. The proceeds would be donated to the Sailors', Soldiers' and Airmens' Comforts Fund. Clark was to see that Nuisance had a good brush-down and, for once, the dog would be expected to wear his rating's cap again.

Three days afterwards Clark, with Nuisance on a chain leash, reported to the CO's office just after noon. The CO's personal car and driver were waiting by the admin block, a miniature white ensign flying at one of the mudguards, denoting it was a British Navy vehicle.

The CO emerged from the admin building dressed in officer's white tropical uniform, cap and shoulder boards glittering with gold braid. He sat beside his driver in the front while Clark and Nuisance rode in the rear seats.

Arriving at the large bungalow-type home with its spacious gardens the CO looked at the crowd which included leading functionaries of the City Council. He had a quiet word with Clark about Nuisance being kept under control during the proceedings, just as his hostess arrived to greet them.

Nuisance, as usual, was loath to show affection to a female, but Clark managed to coax the canine AB to offer his paw to the lady for a handshake. But when she tried to cuddle the massive dog, he pulled so strongly on the leash to escape her attentions that the hefty killick was dragged in another direction.

There were a quartet of musicians on the lawn and, as the CO approached a raised dais, followed by Clark, Nuisance and his hostess, the band started to play the British national anthem. Nuisance, like all humans present, stood 'at attention', black snout in an upraised position, tail stuck out horizontal to the ground, not wagging, ears perked, till the last notes of the tune.

The CO then gave a short address of welcome to all present and thanked them for his invitation – and that of Nuisance too.

There was a large marquee tent and Clark, with his canine oppo, wandered in there. Several women stood behind a long trestle table covered with a snowy tablecloth. There were several dozen dishes containing buffet snacks, a large crystal glass bowl of punch and, on the floor at the end of the table, several cases of lager and liquors. Wine glasses and beer steins were also set out on the table for the convenience of visitors.

One of the women offered Clark a bottle of lager and a beer glass. He gratefully accepted, then asked if Nuisance could have a bottle too. She was delighted to grant his request and poured the drink in a large bowl and placed it on the floor.

All the women watched in amazement as Nuisance finished off the drink in about ten seconds, then laughed as he sat up and begged for more. Another drink was poured for him, which he slurped up neatly and quickly. Then Clark picked up one of the sandwiches which had roast beef between the bread slices, but Nuisance took it in his jaws, laid it on the grass, and delicately used his right paw to remove the top slice. He gulped the meat, leaving all the bread on the turf. He disposed of about a dozen sandwiches in this fashion then begged for another lager, which was provided.

The afternoon passed pleasantly, only spoiled for Nuisance by the attentions of both men and women who constantly tried to make a fuss of this now-legendary AB.

Then the catastrophe occurred which was to be a talking point of civilians and naval ratings in Cape Town and Simon's Town for weeks to come. It also earned him the severe displeasure of his CO.

Several of the visitors had brought their own pets along with them, but not wishing to have them scampering about among other guests, their hostess had provided a haven in a large summer-house at one corner of the garden where they were tied by their leads. One unwise, but genteel, lady thought it was time her pet had a stroll, and fetched the animal on its leash. It was a small pekingese and promptly escaped, making its way towards Nuisance who, led by Clark, was ambling round the garden.

The yapping little pooch suddenly appeared behind the Great Dane and snapped at Nuisance's hind legs.

The canine AB whirled to face this miniature gladiator, gave one ear-shattering bark, bounded forward, snatching the chain leash from the killick's grasp, and set off in pursuit of the tormentor. Most of the genteel ladies began screaming in fright. Though they'd heard Nuisance was harmless to humans, they were afraid they would see the destruction of a lap-dog that would hardly have been a snack for the huge able seaman.

Unfortunately the peke made for the marquee and disappeared inside the tent's doorway. Nuisance, in his haste, caught a leg on a guy rope peg, and the flapping canvas door collapsed. By the time Clark got inside all the women helpers had fled in haste, the little animal had taken refuge behind two close-packed crates of beer while Nuisance, using one of his forepaws, was trying to reach it.

Then the peke darted out and raced under the trestle table, the Great Dane growling and rumbling in excitement at the chase. Nuisance followed but his enormous frame wasn't made for dodging between trestle legs, and he toppled the lot, crockery and food scattering to the ground.

The small dog vanished while Nuisance was covered by the white tablecloth. After he untangled himself he found his prey gone. The crystal punch bowl had somehow miraculously landed the right way up with most of the liquid left in it so, by the time Clark got to him and grabbed his oppo's leash, Nuisance was lapping thirstily at the punch.

Then the CO appeared inside the tent and started delivering the kind of language more consistent with ratings than that of a senior naval officer. This was directed both at Clark, who was rolling about helplessly with laughter, and Nuisance busy with his liquid aperitif. The CO made his apologies to the startled and angry hostess and promised to make good any damage from *Afrikander*'s mess funds. He suggested it would be best if they departed. She agreed emphatically – and the CO, Clark and Nuisance left the premises with their tails between their legs.

Once in the car driving back to Simon's Town, Clark and Nuisance in the back seat, the CO turned to face the broadly-grinning killick. "Clark, it's nothing to laugh about. A bloody disgrace, both to myself and the Royal Navy. Why didn't you take a proper hold on Nuisance's leash?"

"I'm very sorry sir, but have you ever tried to hold Nuisance when he wants to break away . . . it needs at least two men. Besides sir, this is the fourth party we've attended and the first time he's ever caused trouble."

"And it will be the last, Clark. No more parties for that damned AB."

"With respect sir, it wasn't Nuisance's fault. If that lady hadn't fetched her pekingese out it wouldn't have happened. Even if Nuisance had caught him he wouldn't have harmed the little bugger sir, he was only playing about like."

The CO turned once again to face Clark and, to the killick's surprise, was grinning. The naval officer slapped his own knee and guffawed, "Funniest bloody thing I've seen in years Clark; did you see the faces of some lady guests when Nuisance took off? I was thinking of stopping Nuisance's bones for a week, but have decided not to – after all he, like yourself, can't be expected to act with the decorum of an officer and a gentleman."

The CO laughed again. Then Clark said: "With respect sir, you know the old saying from Lord Nelson's days about officers and ratings?"

"No Clark, please enlighten me."

"Well sir, Nelson himself used to say (after he'd won a battle) to his sailors, 'Aft, the most honour, forrard the most glory,' sir. Meaning he knew that, but for the ordinary seamen, there'd have been no victory if they hadn't fought like demons."

"Quite true Clark, and the same holds good today – do the ratings still believe that?"

"Most of them do sir, but I should think Nuisance believes every word of it."

That ended the conversation, with Nuisance never again attending a party – though Clark maintains to this day that Nuisance hated them, anyway.

There are several fallacies and rumours about Nuisance which exist even today. For instance, the belief that he knew when the last trains were due to depart from stations – and that he was familiar with the different times of trains on Saturdays and Sundays. Remember that Nuisance was a dog, albeit an unusually intelligent one, but he could not look at a clock and tell the time. Nor could he differentiate between Saturdays and Sundays.

How he did ascertain train departure times is logical. His instincts told him that when big parties of ratings made their way to the railway station it was time he left too. In just the same way, as he saw ratings going toward the galley at *Afrikander*, he knew it was meal-times.

There are hundreds of accounts of Nuisance leading drunken ratings aboard their ships, which is true. But many other anecdotes are also genuine – where he led a sailor from Cape Town to Simon's Town, when he was not stationed at any of those bases. Clark informs me that in one week Nuisance led seven men to his billet, none of whom were stationed there. But one fact remains indisputable – while in Nuisance's care, they were safe from harm.

I am sorry to disillusion believers of some rumours, but although many of us loved this canine AB as we would a brother, intelligence and canine wisdom should not be confused with fallacies.

The Nelson Touch

In early November 1942 I arrived in Table Bay, Cape Town, aboard a liner of the Chieftain Class, in a convoy with several other troop-carrying ships, most of them taking British troops and airmen to Bombay, India.

My three companions were Fleet Air Arm pilots, one a lieutenant and the other two sub-lieutenants. All we knew was that our destination was a Royal Naval air station named *HMS Malagas* a few miles from Cape Town. On disembarking we reported to the Senior Naval Officer in Cape Town Dockyard who informed us that a lorry from RNAS Wingfield at Goodwood, six miles from town, was on the way to pick us up.

The lorry duly arrived, a three-tonner, canvas-covered. We slung our cases in the back, climbed in and sat on the wooden seats.

Twenty minutes láter we arrived at the aerodrome's main entrance, showed our identity cards to the naval sentries guarding the double iron-barred gates, and the lorry set off up a tarmac road. We passed several buildings on the way, brick walled with plenty of windows and gable roofs of tiles. About half a mile from the gate we arrived at an H-shaped double-storey building with the same brick walls, large windows and a swing-door of anti-mosquito steel mesh.

As I jumped down from the back of the lorry I nearly fell over a massive Great Dane who was walking past in the company of a naval rating dressed in square-rig. I could see by the propeller on his jumper sleeve that he was an air mechanic first class (engines). On the last day of leave at my home, five weeks previously, at the pub door of which my father was the landlord, I had said farewell to a Great Dane puppy six months old which dad had bought to replace our Alsatian which had died of old age, after acting as guard dog to the pub premises for many years. The local postmaster bred Great Danes and had let father have the puppy in exchange for a free pint at our pub, every time he brought our mail.

I had become quite fond of this young dog in the few weeks we'd owned him, and damned if here was a dog of the same breed — but the biggest I had ever seen, with scars all over his body . . . not surprising that I decided to become friendly with this animal. It was not just coincidence, but a logical reaction on my part towards a breed of dog which was already a part of my family.

I moved forward and grasped the massive hound by the big leather collar circling its neck, then stepped quickly back as the dog halted and looked me up and down. The great jaws opened and he gave a low growl, yawned, and started to walk away.

So I turned to the air mechanic and said:

"Excuse me, air mechanic, what is your name."

"Air Mechanic Thomas," he replied.

"That's a fine-looking dog you have there, Air Mechanic Thomas — I have a young Great Dane of my own back home."

"Bless you, he ain't mine; doesn't belong to anybody, this dog; famous all round Cape Town, Simon's Town, and Wingfield. Able Seaman Nuisance is his name; proper seaman in the Royal Navy he is. Look at his identity disc on his collar — official number, rank and name, and a free pass to ride on trains."

I took the disc in my hand and confirmed what the air mechanic had said, but the dog turned to look at me, shook his body and pulled away. I glanced at Thomas, noticing that my three companions had disappeared inside the officers' quarters. But I was curiously excited, and wished to know more.

I was determined to become friendly with this huge dog and asked Thomas:

"Why is he so unfriendly, air mechanic; doesn't seem to want me to pat him?"

"Two reasons, besides him not liking his collar buckled on. Most times one of us will take it off so he's more comfortable like, not very often he wears it nowadays. Second reason is — he doesn't go much on sailors who don't wear square rig. Third, there's a NAAFI canteen that'll be open any minute now, and the manageress gives him a quart of lager and a bone about this time every day. That's where he's heading for now."

"You mean he doesn't like fore-and-aft-rig, Thomas?"

"Like isn't quite the word; he just pays no attention to anybody not dressed as a rating. That includes chiefs, petty officers, and even air fitters, because they all wear fore-and-aft rig." *(Air fitters were of the same section of the Fleet Air Arm as air mechanics, but were considered to be slightly more technical in engineering, and were accordingly dressed as tradesmen of the Royal Navy, that is in fore-and-aft rig.)*

"Then there isn't much chance of me becoming friendly with him?" I asked.

"Not much. I'll give you an idea of what I mean. My billet is about three hundred yards away, about a dozen billets all within a few yards of one another, with shower rooms and heads to one side. Last night Nuisance slept by my bunk. There are 30 of us in each billet. Half are air fitters the other half air mechanics, and there'll be an air fitter next to an air mechanic right through the room — not all fitters in one part of the room and mechanics in another, see what I mean?"

"I understand Thomas, but what's that got to do with the dog sleeping in there?"

"Nuisance will sleep only by an air mechanic's bed. If an air fitter tries to put him by his bed, Nuisance will shove his head at the chap and push him away. But he won't bite anyone, not Navy men anyhow — never been known to yet, though there are rumours that he's been close to it a time or two, when a matelot's been a bit rough to him.''

"Mind if I walk with you to the NAAFI Thomas, I'd like to see the dog have his meal?''

"No, but I should keep well away from him when he's supping his ale and gnawing his bone; doesn't like interruptions when he's feeding.''

Thomas walked up to Nuisance who had stopped and stood with one front paw upraised, looking fed-up with having to wait for his escort. Thomas unbuckled Nuisance's collar, and the dog's tail wagged like a double-time metronome. There was no doubt he hated having to wear a collar.

Thomas, swinging the collar in his hand, walked towards a long, low brick building that had patio-style glass windows and a side entrance with NAAFI painted on the lintel. Nuisance was already squatting on his haunches waiting.

The door suddenly opened and a buxom, motherly-looking woman in her late thirties or early forties, dressed in the dark blue uniform of all NAAFI staff, appeared and placed a large copper bowl on the ground and a haunch of meat beside it. She patted Nuisance's head, but the dog ducked away from her hand. She waved at us and went back inside.

Thomas grinned at me, then said:

"See that, can't stand any kind of women, even if they feed him; we've about 30 Wrens on this station, all of 'em have tried to make friends with him, but it's like a waste of time. He just walks away from them. Likes his own kind of girl-friends, though — Great Dane bitches I mean — married to a pair of them, whether it's legal I don't know, but I've seen a photograph of Nuisance with one of his wives at a wedding they laid on for him.

Tell you something else, he's the only member of the Royal Navy that's excused wearing a cap. That order came straight from the Naval C-in-C.''

I looked at Nuisance in disbelief. Excused wearing a cap — there was a precedent, if you like! Nuisance had lapped up half the lager and now started on the bone. He lay full-length with the bone held firmly between his huge paws and was tearing strips of meat from it, a low growl rumbling when a piece of the flesh refused to be torn away for a second or two. Five minutes later the bone was lying on the ground, picked as clean as if a flock of vultures had been at it.

Nuisance's long, wide tongue lapped up the rest of the lager. He trotted over to Thomas, sat down and held up his right paw. Thomas shook it and I, too, tried but the dog gave one thunderous "Whoof" and ran away.

"What about his collar?'' I asked Thomas.

"I'll leave it with the guardroom sentries. Sometimes they'll put it back on him when he gets in from wherever he's off to now; other times they won't bother. Only reason he wears it at all is that, when he travels on trains, his free pass is tied on the ring. Had a lot of bother with the South African Railways at the start of the war about travelling without a ticket, but they all know him now. The ticket-collectors, I mean — nearly killed

Just Nuisance, wearing forage cap, at RNAS (Royal Naval Air Station) Wingfield, *where he spent part of his naval career. In the background is a Fairey Fulmar aircraft of the Fleet Air Arm.*

one of them when he tried to throw a bulldog pal of Nuisance's off the train."

"You mean he travels on trains all by himself Thomas? How the hell does he know which train to catch and where to get off?"

"Makes no difference to Nuisance, catches the first train that comes along at Goodwood station. It'll be going either to Cape Town or Simon's Town, and Nuisance knows every station over the whole 25 miles between them — probably won't see him again for a week or ten days back here at Wingfield."

"Where does he get to during that time Thomas?"

"In the naval barracks or aboard one of the ships in Simon's Town. Or he might stay at the Union Jack Club in Cape Town or on a ship at the dockyard there. Depends where he thinks the most grub will be or lager to drink. There's a special bed for him at the Union Jack Club, and he's friends of all the big brass, including our CO Captain Farquhar, Commander Shakespear at Simon's Town, and the Port Captain at Cape Town, plus all the chief cooks at every naval base round here.

"I'll bet you that Nuisance is the best-fed and most well-looked-after rating in all South Africa, or in the whole Royal Navy come to that.

"I once heard Captain Farquhar say to the Flying Commander, who you'll be meeting soon, I expect, Nuisance is the nearest thing he'd ever seen to Lord Nelson — ignores officer classes and other superiors like chiefs and petty officers — a real oppo to all seamen, those dressed in square-rig I mean. And, like Nelson, he'll 'turn a blind eye' to anything or anyone he doesn't like. That's what our CO said to the commander.

"You'll get to know more about him quickly, when you've been here a week or so. He's a bloody miracle, is that dog, more sense than most of us in the 'Andrew'. Got to be off now."

I was fortunate in the quarters allocated to me — only this one, and another at the far side of the block, had a door that led directly outside to the narrow grass walkway surrounding the building. This exit door was to be of inestimable help to me in future months, in my efforts to become a companion to Nuisance.

I was soon comfortably settled in my "cabin" and learnt from others that Wingfield was a wonderful place for entertainment facilities. There was a cinema open every night to officers and ratings, with three different films showing each week. The open-air swimming pool was kept spotlessly clean by gangs of Cape Coloureds employed on the aerodrome for all kinds of labouring duties, some working in the ratings' dining hall, others stoking boiler-room fires for constant hot water, others pushing our planes in and out of the hangers.

And once a week we were allowed to take a small jeep-type van by signing it out on a rota system for a period of 24 hours.

I also learnt that, except for emergencies, we would make only one flight every morning of about five hours duration round the approaches to the Cape sea-lanes — spotting for convoys and any U-boats reported in the area, carrying bombs and depth charges in our Albacore aircraft (torpedo-bomber-reconnaisance planes).

The preceding few pages may seem inconsequential in a book about Nuisance, but it is essential that my first meeting with the dog is accurately described — and what motivated my determination to make friends with him. ·

Three days after arriving at Wingfield a sub-lieutenant pilot in my squadron, on hearing that I had not visited Cape Town for shore leave, offered to show me round the town, the hotels, restaurants, city hall, and the botanical gardens at the top of Adderley Street.

We left at lunch-time and caught the train to Cape Town, having had one drink at the Goodwood Hotel opposite the entrance to Wingfield.

My friend was meeting his girl-friend at five that evening so, having shown me round town, I thanked him and he left. About six I was having a snort in the George Hotel, chatting to a South African army captain, when two chief petty officers walked in. From the badges on their jacket collars I could tell they were Fleet Air Arm men, and turned towards them as I heard them mention Nuisance.

Apparently they'd just left the Standard Hotel, where the dog was on the upper balcony watching people below. Hurriedly finishing my drink, I waved cheerio to the captain and set off for the Standard.

I'd only just got out of the doorway of the George when I heard the ear-splitting bark of a dog and knew immediately who it was.

As I neared the Standard I could see people — civilians, sailors, soldiers, and even a few Wrens — laughing and pointing up at the great head of Nuisance poking over the top of the balcony railing.

I went inside and one of the waiters, in answer to my question, pointed to the stairs. I arrived on the balcony to find several people seated at the tables smiling and laughing at the figure of the Great Dane reared up on his hind legs, his forepaws resting on the rail and the gigantic tail swinging madly from side to side. He wasn't wearing a collar. I approached him and stroked his head gently. He turned, looked at me, dropped to all fours, moved along the balcony away from where I stood, then assumed his former position looking down on the street below.

Not a very auspicious beginning to try to make friends, I mused.

I thought for a moment, then went downstairs to the bar. The manager or landlord was serving several ratings who had just entered and, when he'd finished, I asked him if it was possible for him to pour a quart of lager into a large bowl so I could take it to Nuisance.

He picked up what appeared to have been a big chamber-pot and then said: "Sorry, but Nuisance has already had two of these, a quart each time, and some years ago we had a request from your Naval HQ not to get the dog drunk."

"Come on landlord, be a sport, one more quart won't hurt him. My own father is landlord of a pub back in the UK. I was brought up in one; I want to make friends with the dog. Only been here at the Cape for three days."

"Well, just one quart, no more — and he's partial to these meat pies, though I warn you it won't by easy for you.

Nevertheless he filled the pot with a quart of lager, took a meat pie out of a glass cabinet, and I paid him. Carrying the pot in both hands, with the pie stuck in my coat pocket, I climbed to the balcony. This time I used more discretion. Nuisance was still intent on viewing the scene below, so I stopped at a discreet distance, placed the pot on the floor, laid the pie alongside it and seated myself at a vacant table. I called out softly.

"Here Nuisance, lager and big eats."

Hearing his name, Nuisance turned his head and looked straight at me. Then, just as he was showing every indication of ignoring me, his big brown eyes caught sight of the pot and pie.

His floppy ears perked up, then his glance swung between the pot and my face three or four times. I didn't move, though he must have known I'd put the food and drink there. He again looked at the street beneath him and I felt snubbed but, just as I was getting to my feet to leave, Nuisance swung on to all fours, walked to the pot and his large pink tongue began lapping up the lager. After drinking about half, he turned his attention to the meat pie and disposed of it with hardly a gulp. Then he polished off the lager.

As he walked towards the stairs, he stopped by my table and looked me directly in the face. For a moment or two I thought he was going to hold out his paw, as he had done to Air Mechanic Thomas at Wingfield, but some inbred instinct must have warned him that this would mean lowering his sense of values. Lifting his black pug nose skywards, he walked disdainfully past me down the stairs.

As I picked up the empty pot I felt elation. At least he had accepted my offerings. That was a start, anyway.

I took the pot back to the manager who looked somewhat startled. I smiled and murmured:

"We've had a dog in our family ever since I can remember, landlord, and one thing I have learnt about them, they have some sort of sixth sense when it comes to mutual trust and liking between a man and a dog."

"That may well be, but Nuisance is special when it comes to relationships, besides being far more intelligent than any dog I know. Take it from me, that dog was feeling real thirsty — otherwise he wouldn't have touched that lager."

This deflated my feeling of triumph slightly, but made me more determined than ever to gain Nuisance's friendship. Perhaps, by making enquiries of several ratings who knew him well, I could discover the reason why he preferred square-rigged ratings and practically ignored everyone else.

A couple of days after this meeting with Nuisance in Cape Town I found that a maintenance air fitter, Air Mechanic (Engines) Jones, knew Nuisance quite well. The dog had slept by his bed several nights and, also, Jones had been stationed at Wingfield nearly two years and remembered the time Nuisance had first appeared on the aerodrome, about August 1940. I asked him why Nuisance had time only for seamen in square rig, and he answered:

"Nobody really knows, we've just come to accept it as a fact. I've an oppo stationed at Simon's Town, name of Leading Seaman Clark; he's about to be rated as a petty officer, but he's been sort of an escort to the dog since 1940. Probably knows him better than anyone else in the Royal Navy. Told me once that, before Nuisance listed, he belonged to a chap named Chaney who is in charge of the United Services Institute at Simon's Town. He took Nuisance with him when he took over the job, and it was mostly ratings in square rig who used that place.

"Nuisance was only about a year old then, and the sailors that went in there also let him board their ships in the dockyard. They treated him so well — fed him, gave him lager — that he came to look on them as friends. Then two or three petty officers, before Nuisance became well-known and liked, turfed him off the ship. Leading Seaman Clark reckons that's why Nuisance doesn't like chaps dressed in fore-and-aft rig, never mind whether they're officers or petty officers.

"If you're ever in Simon's Town I should look Clark up, if you want to know more about Nuisance."

Soon after, as I'd had trouble with a hollow tooth for some while, I saw our surgeon-commander at Wingfield. As we had no dental surgeon on the aerodrome, he arranged for me to visit the Royal Naval Hospital at Simon's Town which had a fine, well-staffed dental surgery.

The appointment was for next day at 10 and I arrived there in a small van driven by one of the guardroom staff. To my astonishment, I saw Nuisance standing at the top of the steps leading to the entrance. But, as I got nearer, I found I was mistaken. It wasn't Nuisance but another Great Dane quite a bit smaller than the AB. When I mentioned this to the Wren receptionist she smiled:

"You're not far wrong, that's Nuisance's brother. We call him Bats."

I had my tooth drilled and filled, thanked the surgeon and left. As I went out the door Bats placed his body in front of me and refused to allow me down the steps.

I tried walking round him, but he was too quick, and a menacing growl warned me not to proceed further. I went back into the reception hall and explained what the dog was doing.

The Wren smiled and said that was Bats' usual style — he'd allow anyone to enter the hospital but would stop them leaving.

So I asked, "I know that the term Bats in sailors' slang for anyone with bit feet or large ears, but I rather think he must have got the name from the old English saying bats-in-the-belfry — is that so miss?"

"I shouldn't be at all surprised," she answered, then called to a rating who stood by her desk:

"Able Seaman, would you please act as escort past our canine guardian angel?'' And she smiled again.

I followed the able seaman who walked up to Bats, grasped his collar and remarked:

"Got him now, — just walk down the steps.''

I did so but noticed that as I passed Nuisance's brother the dog still tried to escape the seaman's grip to block my way, but the sailor must have been used to his antics and pulled him sharply back.

As I left the base hospital I remembered someone mentioning that Nuisance's previous owner was in charge of the Sailors' and Soldiers' Institute and asked a passing rating the way to it.

I found a middle-aged man reclining on a sort of beach deck-chair, in front of the entrance. Although the door was open, there was no one inside the building. I had the whole day to myself after visiting the dentist and walked over to the man.

"Are you Mr Chaney sir?'' I asked.

"I am, what can I do for you?''

"Well I don't really know for sure sir, but I'm from Wingfield — only been at the Cape a few days, straight from the UK — and I understand you were once the owner of Nuisance. I've met the dog a couple of times and been trying to make friends — you see, my parents and I own a Great Dane puppy back home in the UK, and I'm trying to make friends with Nuisance.

"I think he's the most intelligent and lovable dog I've ever met, besides being the biggest and strongest. I wonder if you can tell me why he has this preference for ratings who wear square rig, and barely notices or acknowledges the presence of us chaps who are dressed fore-and-aft. Can you tell me what he was like when you owned him?''

Chaney smiled, went inside the Institute and came out with a chair, gesturing for me to sit down beside him.

In his opinion the reason why Nuisance preferred square rig was simple. They formed by far the majority of Royal Navy personnel anywhere on the Peninsula and, consequently, the Great Dane received food and lager from men dressed as seamen in far larger quantities than from chaps dressed in fore-and-aft rig.

Also, ratings were inclined to be more jovial and playful with the dog than other more senior ranks.

Evidently Nuisance considered the bell-bottomed sailors to be his best friends and, therefore, his closest oppos. Several ratings had told Chaney that before Nuisance was officially enlisted in the navy, when he'd been taken aboard ships in Simon's Town harbour, some officious petty officers and officers aboard had turfed him off. No rating had ever inflicted this indignity on him. The dog had a remarkable memory — he never forgot a kindness, neither did he forget a slight, many of the latter being accorded him by navy men clad in fore-and-aft uniforms.

During his vendetta with the South African Railways more than two years previously, it was always the ratings who'd helped him. When billeted at Froggy Pond and *HMS Afrikander I* it was always the bell-bottomed sailors who were his bed-fellows. They also took him into Cape Town, to the dining hall for meals, and helped him in many ways. It was nothing surprising that Nuisance had got his priorities right about who he could rely on for the most kindness and help.

Mr Chaney noticed the glum expression I had on my face as he recounted the facts, for he smiled again and told me it wasn't all bad news. Nuisance, in spite of exaggerated rumours to the contrary, did have a few men dressed in fore-and-aft rig whom he regarded as friends and oppos. The chief petty officer cooks, for instance, who provided him with bones, meat, and fresh milk and the occasional quart of lager.

Then there was the surgeon-commander at *Afrikander* — he received as much attention from Nuisance as any rating. After the commander had cured his lameness by clipping the ingrowing nail, whenever the doctor happened to be near Nuisance, the dog would race towards him and hold out a paw to be shaken.

So that was another myth, about the dog having no time for fore-and-aft rig, which simply wasn't true. It applied to a large majority of them, but not all.

Chaney grinned at me and said surely this proved there was some hope for me being able to become pally with Nuisance — but be patient. The surest way to make Nuisance dislike me was to try to lavish unwanted attention on him.

Chaney then related several comical episodes that happened while Nuisance lived with him at Mowbray. Firstly there was the incident about the mutton bone from the refrigerator, which has been described in a previous chapter.

Then, when Mr Chaney had owned Nuisance for a few weeks, he was standing by his front gate when a lorry-load of ratings drove down the road. The sailors were laughing and singing and Nuisance, who was standing at his side, took off like a rocket after the vehicle. He leaped clean over the tail-board, which was about 1,5 m from the roadway, knocking several of them over. The last sight Mr Chaney had of his pet was all of the navy men patting his head and stroking him.

It was lucky that Nuisance was wearing his collar at the time with a disc engraved with his name and home address, otherwise he might have had difficulty in regaining ownership of the dog.

About an hour later a small Royal Navy van had stopped outside his gate while Chaney was telling one of his neighbours about Nuisance's disappearance. A chief petty officer got out the van and he held the runaway by a piece of rope threaded through the collar. The CPO said that Nuisance had become so popular in half an hour, when the lorry arrived at *Afrikander*, that none of the ratings was prepared to return the dog, and claimed he was a stray. It took a direct order from their CO to hand him over to the CPO and, even then, they claimed the dog was starving and begged the biggest bone that could be found in the galley from the chief cook. Nuisance still had the bone gripped in his huge jaws when the petty officer handed him back, but half the meat had already been gnawed from it.

Then there was the day when Mrs Chaney forgot to pour out Nuisance's usual bowl of milk before going out shopping in town. Mr Chaney was writing a letter to a friend in the living room and went into the kitchen a few seconds too late to prevent Nuisance having a painful experience. The dog was thirsty and, having noticed how his master and mistress turned on the water taps at the sink, had placed his forepaws on the sink edge then poked out his right paw and turned on one of the taps. Before Chaney could stop him Nuisance had lapped up some water from the faucet and let out a roar like a salvo of guns. He'd gulped water from the hot water system. Luckily it wasn't boiling — but Nuisance was a coward when it came to suffering in silence.

He leapt down from the sink, made about four circuits of the kitchen at top speed, knocking over the table and two chairs, then ran out of the back door his long tongue held out to catch the cooling breeze that his passage round the garden caused. Then he darted back into the house, while Mr Chaney filled a garden bucket full of cold water with ice cubes in it and Nuisance lapped up the whole lot.

He wandered over to his boss (who swore it was the first time he'd ever seen tears in the dog's eyes), sat down and held out his paw in gratitude.

Chaney laughed and warned me that if ever Nuisance licked me, to make sure it wasn't on my face, as the surface of the tongue was like coarse emery paper. Whenever Nuisance turned on the cold water tap after that, he'd always swipe with one paw at the hot water tap as much as to say:

"I won't forget you, mate!"

Then Benjamin Chaney went on to describe what he called 'the event of Nuisance's guests.' Apparently all one Sunday morning and afternoon the Great Dane had not been seen. Then, about 4.30 as the Chaneys sat on the small stoep of their home, the front gate opened and Nuisance, pulling a rating by his jumper cuff gripped in his mouth, entered the garden. Five other ratings followed, all looking sheepish.

They were welcomed and one of them, a leading seaman who seemed to be in charge of the group (except for Nuisance, of course) explained that the dog had been at *Afrikander* all day and as the six ratings caught the train to Cape Town for an evening out Nuisance had followed them. But when the train arrived near Mowbray the dog had moved among them, tugging their sleeves, indicating he wanted them to accompany him. So they all alighted and followed as he led the way to the Chaneys' house.

After informing them that he was the dog's owner, but not its master, as no one would ever be that, Mr Chaney invited them all into his home saying that Nuisance considered himself as one of the family, not a pet.

Mrs Chaney cooked a sumptuous meal for her six visitors which left her refrigerator nearly bare of food and Chaney, who liked a drink of beer himself, provided each sailor with two-pint bottles of lager. One of the ratings asked if he could use the toilet, but as he rose to go down the passage, Nuisance thought the the rating was preparing to leave without permission.

Nuisance walked over and, standing upright on his hind legs, placed his paws each side of the rating's shoulders and pushed him back on the seat. Chaney finally persuaded Nuisance to relent.

Altogether, they had all had a fine evening — and never had he seen Nuisance in such high spirits, entertaining six naval ratings in his home.

Finally, at the station, as each rating boarded the train Nuisance held out his paw to be shaken. As the train disappeared in the direction of Simon's Town Nuisance stood on the station platform watching the rear lights of the last coach till they were out of sight, his tail wagging very slightly. But as they walked home, the long tail resumed its frantic sweeping motion, indicating he was in his normal good spirits once more and had done his good deed for the day.

This all proved that the dog, like all sailors, had a strong feeling of sentimentality.

Chaney glanced at his watch and said that he had just time to tell me one more story before he had to help his wife in the Institute. This tale, in his opinion, was the most comical of all.

A couple of weeks before Mr Chaney left Mowbray to take up his appointment at the United Services Institute, he was prowling round his garden one night, looking for Nuisance. It was about 10,30 and he wanted to lock up before going to bed. He'd seen Nuisance about an hour before walking round the perimeter fence.

He called and whistled for ten minutes or so and went indoors to wait for the dog to come scratching at the door. It was quite usual for Nuisance to wander about at night and turn up unexpectedly.

Suddenly there was a loud knocking at the front door and, when he opened it, he saw a young man who'd moved into a house three doors away only a few weeks previously. He and his young wife had soon become friendly with the Chaneys.

The young man was in a highly excited state and asked Chaney to come round to his house as Nuisance was there. The neighbour shook his head and said: "Wait until you see where the dog is . . ."

He led Chaney up a short flight of stairs, at his home, opened a door and asked him to look inside.

Obviously it was the young couple's bedroom, and it had a large canopy-type bed with mosquito curtains all round. But a cloud of feathers were floating all round the room and others were scattered about the floor and on the dressing table top, some even clinging to the bed's mosquito netting.

Nuisance was lying on the bed, massive hind legs stretched out towards the foot, both forepaws lying on the pillow, and was snoring lustily. Unfortunately Nuisance's sharp claws had torn one of the pillow covers, and it was from this rent that the feathers were escaping. One of them floated out and landed on the dog's damp nose and Nuisance let out a sneeze that sounded like a train blowing off surplus steam.

Nuisance woke with a start and Chaney stepped over, opened the mosquito net and indicated to the dog that he should get out of bed. Nuisance yawned, as if to say "this is a bit of alright for a kip", and then leapt out and followed his boss down the stairs. Chaney apologised profusely, promising to replace the damaged goose-feather pillow, while Nuisance — realising he had committed an act of vandalism, albeit unintentional — held out his paw for the young man to shake in a canine act of atonement. The young man laughed and shook the profferred paw and, to Chaney's amazement, Nuisance even allowed the man's wife to shake it as well. It was only when he was in a particularly good humour that Nuisance allowed even Mrs Chaney to shake his paw.

When Chaney got home it was a good five minutes before he could stop laughing, while Nuisance stood there, wagging tail in a blur of movement and his large tongue hanging out as if he too was laughing.

The young man's wife later made a habit of bringing round a large bone two or three times a week for Nuisance, but the dog refused to let her shake his paw again. One shake was enough for any female — in the dog's mind a feast — twice would have been gluttony.

I never met Mrs Chaney, and never saw Chaney again, but that one-time owner of Nuisance was a gentleman in every sense of the word. I sincerely hope that he lives, or did live, to a ripe old age — and his good lady, too. I cannot imagine anyone more suited to look after Nuisance other than his subsequent naval oppos.

I saw Nuisance again only a month later — and that was at Wingfield, in most exceptional and unusual circumstances. The aerodrome was surrounded by a chain-link perimeter fence about 3 m in height to keep out unauthorised persons. It covered about four square miles, with the guardroom and a pair of large steel gates as the only entrance and exit. There were hangars for our planes, a mile-long tarmac runway for aircraft take-offs and landings, and the whole vast area was dotted with buildings of all kinds. There were the billets for petty officer ranks and, a mile away from these, a cluster of billets for ratings; the officers' quarters; a large NAAFI, where beer, chocolates and cigarettes were half the prices that ruled in shops of the UK; an indoor cinema and open-air swimming pool, for officers, ratings and wrens, collectively.

There were engine repair shops; ratings' and petty officers' dining halls; but there was plenty of space between all these buildings. Each billet for the ratings held 30 bunks with a large steel clothes locker for each man, and the ratings' quarters were nearly two miles from the main gates of the guardroom. There was a regular transport laid on, at specified hours, to take officers and ratings to the main gates. Here they could, after a short walk, catch a bus or train to Cape Town. A wide tarmac road provided access for this transport. It has been necessary to give this rough indication of the layout to understand how it was possible for the next Nuisance incident to have happened.

The lorry transport for officers and ratings going ashore was a converted low-loader. This was a trailer-type vehicle 12 m long. It had a low chassis which was used for carrying the fuselages and mainplanes of aircraft unloaded at the docks in Cape Town from merchant ships. These were brought to Wingfield for assembly into a completed aircraft. Wooden slat seats had been fixed to each side of this trailer which could take about 60 men.

This particular day two sub-lieutenants and myself, with 40 or so ratings boarded the trailer for the journey to the guardroom. About 400 metres from the gates, built beside the perimeter fence, was an isolated toilet used mostly by sentry patrols checking the fence during darkness. As the transport approached this toilet we could all hear the loud barks of a dog, so loud it only could have been Nuisance. Nearer the toilet building, which was quite small, we saw Nuisance standing by the open door, head in the air, letting go with his ear-shattering barks.

The driver, realising that Nuisance wasn't barking without good reason, stopped the vehicle. A petty officer and two ratings stepped off and walked towards the open door of the toilet. Nuisance gave a final roar and went inside. The three sailors followed and, two seconds later, the petty officer came dashing out and yelled:

"Any sick-bay attendants on this bus? There's an air fitter in there lying on the floor unconscious."

The only sick-bay rating on the trailer hurried into the toilet, poked his head out of the door and waited for the driver to get to the guardroom as quickly as possible to phone for an ambulance. Nuisance elected to stay in the building with his unconscious oppo.

As my chums and I headed out of the gates we heard the sound of the base's ambulance siren whining in the distance.

Around midnight we returned from Cape Town and I asked one of the guardroom staff how the rating was, and what had been wrong with him.

He replied that the medical officer had diagnosed it as a severe case of malaria, as the rating, two days before, had arrived from Freetown, Sierra Leone.

I saw the MO next morning outside the mess and asked him how the air mechanic was. He replied: "Just come from examining him. He'll be OK I believe — but I can tell you this, it was Nuisance who saved his life. Hardly anyone goes in that building except at night and, if he'd been left lying there without medical attention for about five hours more, he'd have been dead by now. I don't know how one recommends a dog for a gong, but I'm certainly going to try to get one for Nuisance."

The doctor did recommend Nuisance for a medal, but it wasn't granted, even though our CO, Captain Farquhar, added his own strong personal plea for an award. However, the Senior Naval Officer, South Atlantic, would not confirm it. He replied, in a signal to Wingfield, that Nuisance already had two precedents to his name — "excused caps" and the only animal to be officially enlisted in the Royal Navy. However he left it to

Captain Farquhar to reward the able seaman in any other way that did not contravene naval regulations.

Our CO promptly awarded Nuisance 14 days leave, double rations of meat and bones, and freedom of the NAAFI supplies, to be rationed out by the manageress at her discretion. Nuisance, from that date, was also excused all ceremonial parades when he had to wear his hated cap and collar.

The CO had memos prepared and posted on all officers' and ratings' notice boards at Wingfield. Our flight commander (who was a friend of the CO) told us in confidence that Captain Farqhuar was extremely angry that a medal had not been awarded the dog, and that he respected and had an affection for Nuisance equal to that of any rating at Wingfield or any other base on the Peninsula. I say, without any reservations, that Captain Farquhar was the finest CO I ever served under, either ashore or at sea during the whole of my naval service.

It is a great pity that Nuisance never knew just how much this naval officer (who was to be promoted an admiral before he retired from the Royal Navy) cared for him.

I can give an instance of this. Nuisance, a few days after the above incident, somehow found his way into the officers' wardroom, when only a few junior officers were present. They were feeding slices of meat to him and letting him sup from a bottle of lager when the wardroom president came in. A full commander, and a very strict disciplinarian. The only ratings allowed in the wardroom were officer's stewards who served drinks and meals. Chiefs and petty officers were barred, too. Even our CO had to ask the commander's permission to enter as, strictly speaking, he was not a member — although any officer of the Royal Navy, Army, or Royal Air Force, could be invited in as a guest of any member.

The commander glanced at Nuisance, glared at the junior officers who were feeding him and giving him lager, and called for a number of officers' stewards to eject the intruder. The commander's yells were so loud that our CO, who had a private room just down the corridor from the wardroom, suddenly appeared and asked:

"May I be admitted to the wardroom commander?"

"Of course sir, it's my privilege to ask you to be our guest."

"What is all the commotion commander? I'm sure I heard someone shouting very loudly in here a short while ago."

"That was me sir, Able Seaman Nuisance was being entertained in this room by these junior officers, all air-crew officers who have no idea of protocol or discipline."

"With respect commander, these junior officers happen to be the reason for our presence here, and their rank is irrelevant. I agree that this able seaman is contravening regulations by his presence in the wardroom, but that is no reason to subject commissioned pilots to derogatory remarks. I suggest they deserve an apology."

The commander's face was flushed with anger, but he turned, bowed briefly and murmured:

"Please accept my apologies gentlemen. I didn't mean to offend you."

The CO looked at the commander and said:

"And, commander, I also suggest that you appreciate that this is no ordinary rating — it's only a few days ago that he saved the life of a rating under my command. Although he is exceedingly clever, he cannot read the notice outside which specifies who may or may not enter your wardroom. I make it my personal responsibility that he be allowed in the precincts of these officers' quarters at any time.

"Call him my personal servant if you wish to maintain regulations. I cannot, and will not, insist that his presence be allowed in the wardroom; but the chief petty officer steward has his own quarters behind the bar. Is that not so, CPO? Will you allow this seaman to be your assistant steward, on a temporary basis, of course?"

"Certainly sir," replied the CPO and, with a smile on his face, our CO left.

The commander was still very red in the face and, glaring at the junior officers once more, strode out. The CPO steward, with a huge grin on his face, led Nuisance to his private cubby hole, behind the bar where drinks were served.

Our CO thought as much of the canine able seaman as he ever would of any naval officer on the base although, except for such occasions described above, he was at great pains to appear strictly impartial. He may have fooled many executive officers, (non-aircrew) chiefs, petty officers and ratings, but his high regard and affection for Nuisance was common knowledge among our young pilots. If you ask me how we knew this I can say only that it was the CO's manner towards the dog. It was akin to the feeling of comradeship between pilots serving in the same squadron. Nuisance could have no higher accolade bestowed on him than the friendship of such an officer who embodied the highest traditions of the Royal Navy.

Aircrew Observer

In the early months of 1943, after an absence of two or three weeks from Wingfield, Nuisance turned up on the aerodrome again. I had seen him several times at various places in town but, remembering Chaney's word about patience if I wanted the dog to regard me as a friend, had not tried to contact him. Particularly as he was always in the company of his square-rigged oppos.

One Sunday evening, however, I heard a lieutenant RN (not Fleet Air Arm) who had apparently been duty officer that day, laughing loudly at an incident he was relating to three pilots and two other executive officers.

Every Sunday morning there was a ceremonial parade on the drill ground of the aerodrome, known as Sunday morning divisions and church parade. Nuisance had been excused from these Sunday occasions by our CO for some months now. Every officer, chief, petty officer and rating on the base had to attend. The only ones excused were the sweepers – that is, one rating from each billet who swept out the floors, cleaned the windows, picked up the debris surrounding the billets and so on.

The CO was always present, and the different religious denominations each attended their own service. Roman Catholics in the cinema, for their church communion; Church of England in the dining hall; Church of Scotland in the NAAFI. The Royal Navy insisted that all men should belong to some recognised denomination for religious services. It was no good claiming to be an agnostic or atheist. When any man enlisted, he was always endowed with some religious denomination.

These Sunday morning parades were unpopular, especially among the ratings, for a variety of reasons. Firstly, it meant they had to rise just as early as on a weekday; secondly, they had to wear their smartest uniforms and be clean-shaven, as the CO was quite prone to hold a quick inspection of all ranks, including officers.

Few sailors were religious and they were mostly bored with the church services they had to attend. Because of this many of them used to hide on the outskirts of the aerodrome or in some vacant building, some in the hangars or even in the cockpits of aircraft. The only trouble was that the master-at-arms had his men out in patrol jeeps trying to catch anyone who had missed divisions. Those caught appeared before their divisional officers and were automatically awarded seven days stoppage of leave and pay.

Apparently this duty officer, with three men of the MAA's staff, had been looking for men hiding in the vicinity of billets at the most remote corner of the base.

They entered one billet, noted that only the sweeper was present and were just preparing to emerge when there was a loud splintering crash from the roof. Then there was a bark of rage that could have been heard miles away. They all knew who it was, Nuisance!

The officer looked up at the white-washed boards that formed the ceiling, and a large forepaw was dangling through a splintered gash near a trapdoor that gave access to the loft above.

All billet huts were brick-built with windows along each side, and a tiled gable-shaped roof. Large cross-timbers about 1,5 m apart formed the fixing points for the ceiling boards. Each billet also had a long trestle table in the space between each row of bunks. Here ratings ironed their shirts and other parts of their uniforms. The officer snatched a sweeping broom leaning against one wall, climbed on the table and pushed the handle against the trapdoor so it lifted from its recess. While he was doing this Nuisance was letting out lion-like noises. The officer yelled up into the loft for all ratings hiding there to come down.

Ten ratings lowered themselves to the table, followed by two more who had extricated Nuisance's forepaw from the broken board. Then six ratings helped to lift Nuisance down. He was unhurt, except for a small graze on his right forepaw. He had stopped barking and the officer lined all the truants up in the centre of the room. He later related that Nuisance waited till they were all in line and joined the last man of the file. His tail was swinging to and fro, and one of the regulating staff explained to the officer that Nuisance was excused divisions and had not committed an offence. The officer tried to pull Nuisance away from the 12 ratings who had infringed regulations, but the dog refused to be moved from his oppos. If they were in trouble, he was. If they were going to be given a reward, he wanted to share in it.

The officer desisted in his efforts to move Nuisance and asked one of the hideaways what had happened. The rating was honest. They had deliberately hidden so that they could avoid Sunday morning divisions. They had climbed up in the loft and each man had sat on one of the cross-beams, knowing that the thin plywood would not support their weight.

Nuisance had been in the billet all night and insisted on accompanying them into the loft. Unfortunately just as the search party were leaving, the huge Great Dane had shifted from the beam they'd placed him on and put his full weight on the plywood, which gave way.

The officer took the names of all 12 for being adrift from divisions and, although he did not like doing it, had to put Nuisance's name down, too, for damaging Admiralty property – to wit, one billet ceiling board.

All of us were rolling about in hilarious glee at this tale and the duty officer was nearly in hysterics, too – after all, he'd seen it!

All 12 ratings, and Nuisance, were to appear on defaulter's parade the next morning, which would be presided over by the "first lieutenant," a lieutenant-commander.

Only five minutes later, too soon to be a coincidence, our CO was in the mess and asked the duty lieutenant what trouble had Nuisance got into now. After listening for a couple of minutes he chuckled and said that, as so many ratings were involved, he would take defaulters' parade himself next morning. I would have bet a month's pay that if Nuisance got off lightly so would the 12. Our CO was strictly impartial, to rating or dog.

The next day I asked the divisional officer, whose duty it was to attend defaulters' parade, what had transpired.

The DO grinned and replied that all 12 ratings had escaped with a caution, and the CO had turned to the master-at-arms when Nuisance had appeared before him with his cap on, so that the order "off caps" could be given.

"Master, I fail to understand why this rating was charged at all. He is excused Sunday divisions, was obviously enticed into the loft by his shipmates, the ceiling board was broken by accident. It was not a deliberate attempt to damage Admiralty property. In my opinion there is no case to answer, the accused is dismissed with no punishment and the charge is deleted from his conduct sheet."

The DO then remarked it was the first time he'd ever seen the MAA smile while taking defaulters' parade – he had even tied Nuisance's cap back on himself.

Nuisance when at Wingfield showed in many ways how sensible he was. He had the free run of the aerodrome, but never once did I see him on the runway where our planes took off and landed. It was as if he knew this was a dangerous spot to be, probably because no sailors, either, ever walked on the long tarmac-covered airstrip.

Sometimes he appeared in the hangars where maintenance crews were working on our planes, checking for faults on engines, electrical equipment, airframe fuselages and armoury (guns and bomb release mechanisms). Occasionally one of the engine fitters would start an engine for a test run.

When this happened when Nuisance was in the hangar his ears would jerk upright, wagging tail assuming a vertical, motionless position. He'd utter a series of barks, drowned by the terrific noise of the engine, then tuck his tail between his legs and leave the hangar at full speed. I think he was a bit jealous that anything could make a louder noise than he could . . . .

Eventually the mechanics used to lead him outside the hangar before starting the engines.

Also, whenever a plane took off on a flight when Nuisance was wandering round the base he would take up a position where he could see the aircraft taxiing along the runway, standing with his right forepaw raised off the ground, tail wagging with excitement, his eyes following the machine bound for the sky. When it lifted off, he'd raise his pug nose and make a series of little leaps with his front paws and watch the plane till it disappeared from view.

Strangely, when an aircraft was landing he paid no heed at all.

I saw these reactions three or four times before a thought struck me. How would Nuisance react to a flight in a plane? Would he be air-sick? This often happened to pilots and air-gunners who had hundreds of flying hours to their credit. It had also afflicted me a couple of times. However, to get him airborne I had to have the assistance of the maintenance crew and, most of all, the TAG (telegraphist air-gunner) in the plane.

These men were usually killicks or petty officers; they were responsible for all radio communications with base control – and the rear guns. Two forward machine guns were mounted on the lower fuselage, fired by the pilot by depressing a button on the control joystick. The TAG was a leading naval airman, dressed in Nuisance's preferred square rig uniform.

It is necessary to briefly describe an Albacore aircraft to gain a rough idea of what it was used for. Basically it was a reconnaissance torpedo bomber. It could carry bombs or depth-charges for attacking U-boats, or a single large torpedo if used to attack enemy shipping. The torpedo was slung directly under the central fuselage. The cockpit, with a perspex canopy cover, could carry three aircrew – pilot, observer, and TAG. As there was no enemy shipping round the Cape we never carried a torpedo, just bombs and depth charges. Neither did we have an observer on patrol flights as this gave us extra range without his weight – but there was always a safety margin of petrol for the limit of our search area. This would be enough to make up for the presence of Nuisance in the cockpit.

The problem was how to get him into the cockpit without being seen . . .

The TAG was a bit concerned when I put the idea to him – not for himself, but for the pilot. He said it would be a court-martial affair if the pilot was caught taking Nuisance on a flight, an operational one at that.

The pilot had a little conference with his four maintenance crew. Being ratings they were delighted at the idea but, like the TAG, a bit worried about the pilot escaping detection. They were a very loyal bunch of matelots.

One of them, a leading air mechanic, took the pilot's sleeve and murmured: "I think I've got an idea how we can get Nuisance aboard without him being spotted sir. We'll have to tie him down in some way so he doesn't lift his head while you take off and the chaps in the control tower can't see. If we put his collar on and make him lie down beneath the observer's seat, his hind legs can stretch back towards the TAG's part of the cockpit. Then we can tie a piece of rope to the collar, lash it low down near the floor – and you can let him go once you're out at sea. Not before – he could be seen by ground observers scattered round the coast, army gunners for instance."

"That's a good idea killick", the pilot replied, "but how do we get him in the cockpit?"

"Easy sir. Who pushes the plane out of the hangar ready for take-off, and when do you and the TAG climb aboard?"

"Why, the men we employ as airfield labourers. About a dozen or so wheel it out of the hangar and line it up ready for me to taxi for take-off, and one of you chaps sits in the cockpit to see everything's going all right.''

"Correct sir, and as the perspex cockpit is about ten feet off the ground the labourers can't see who's inside. We'll make them all move off out of the hangar till Nuisance is strapped in. I'll climb in myself and hold him down and then, when you land again, we'll do the whole thing in reverse. You and the TAG will climb out on the tarmac outside the hangar, having strapped Nuisance down again just before you hit the coast on your return. The labourers will push the plane back in the hangar. We clear them off, fetch Nuisance and, even if they see the dog walk out of the hangar, nobody can prove a thing."

We agreed on this idea and, as the Albacore was due for early-morning patrol next day, decided to try out the idea then. The leading air mechanic would keep Nuisance by his bed all night, then next morning put the dog's collar on, which was kept in the guardroom, and take the Great Dane into the hangar, clear out the labourers till the dog was safely strapped in – then wheel the kite out.

It worked like a charm.

The air crew arrived in the little van that had fetched them from their billets, already wearing flying gear. The Albacore stood outside the hanger with the prop idling, warming up the engine. The killick was seated in the pilot's chair and he grinned and held up both thumbs in triumph, then climbed down from the plane.

Nuisance was lying flat in the observer's position. After plugging in his wireless and putting the ear-phones on his head, the pilot requested the control tower for permission to take off. This was given and the Albacore sped down the runway and lifted into the sky.

Five minutes later it crossed the Cape coast and, over the intercom, the pilot asked the TAG to release Nuisance.

The dog reared up and placed both paws on the base of the perspex canopy, looked down at the sea below, then at the white cumulus clouds overhead – and, even through his earphones, the pilot could hear his ecstatic barking. His tail was one swishing blur of speed, thumping against the back of the observer's seat.

The pilot turned round and stroked his head – and a miracle happened. He looked back with eyes that seemed twice as large as normal, licked the pilot's gloved hand and gave another resounding bark of ecstasy.

He was certainly immune to air-sickness, at least on this his maiden flight, and as the Albacore flew lower over the sea his head was swinging in all directions. Up, down, to the right, then the left, his whole body quivering with excitement. He behaved impeccably during the whole five-hour flight. I had been a little scared that he might try to move round the confined space and perhaps interfere with control of the aircraft, but he hardly moved, except when nearly at the end of the outward journey a large convoy of merchant ships with five destroyers as escort vessels heading for the Cape, was sighted.

From the lead destroyer an Aldis signalling lamp blinked and the TAG took down the Morse code message, then spoke over the intercom.

"Skipper, message reads: 'From Senior Officer Destroyers to Fleet Air Arm patrol. From what date did the Royal Navy allow animals to act as aircrew?' "

The pilot felt the sweat break out all over him. If this senior officer reported the sight of Nuisance when he arrived in Cape Town, the pilot was in serious trouble. He'd forgotten all about Nuisance since coming within range of the convoy, so he spoke on the intercom.

"TAG use your own Aldis lamp and make this reply. 'To Senior Officer Destroyers from Fleet Air Arm patrol – With respect sir, he's my large toy mascot.' "

Two minutes later the destroyer's Aldis started winking again and the TAG reported the message read.

"Senior Officer Destroyers to Fleet Air Arm patrol pilot. Query as to toy mascot, must have been dust speck on my binoculars, I see no animal now, many thanks for your air cover, message ends. Good luck."

The pilot clapped his hands in relief, but quickly grasped the joystick again as the Albacore started to bank sideways, regained control of the machine and spoke into the intercom.

"That destroyer skipper wasn't fooled for a minute. He knew it was a real dog. Thank God he was a decent sort. He'll not report anything about Nuisance being aboard, or he'd have left me in no doubt as to what would happen to me when he docks in Table Bay. Next time we have Nuisance aboard and sight a convoy, remind me to pull him down from the canopy.''

''Aye, aye sir, but you should have seen Nuisance when he saw all those ships below, he was bouncing his head up and down, as if he was spotting every single one of them. I reckon he knows there's plenty of his oppos down there''.

The Albacore arrived back at Wingfield and taxied to the hangar. The pilot and TAG climbed out of the aircraft and the labourers shoved it into its parking area. Then the mechanics sent them packing while Nuisance was lifted out. I looked inside and Nuisance was running round the hangar like a greyhound after a rabbit, stopping now and again to snap at his own tail. The pilot laughed and called. The dog rushed over, placed his paws on his shoulders and as he removed his flying helmet, he licked his cheek. Although delighted at Nuisance's gesture of affection, Chaney was right – the dog's tongue was as rough as emery cloth. Nuisance then raced off, but every now and again as he disappeared from sight he bounded into the air as if he would have liked to leave for the sky again.

Another precedent set, I thought. An able seaman as an aircrew observer – standards in the Fleet Air Arm were definitely changing . . .

The leading air mechanic came towards the pilot grinning and chuckling. ''How did it go sir? No one suspects anything here.''

The pilot told him everything had been fine, then related the incident about the destroyer captain and his eyes widened and he whistled, ''He must have been a good sport sir. If he'd reported you, there'd have been a real heap of bother on your plate.''

''I hope I meet him one day killick, and I'll buy him the best meal and treat him to every drink he wants to swallow, even if I spend the last penny in my pocket. By the way, I don't intend to try this too often – perhaps once every three months or so. Thank your mates for me, and there'll be half a dozen bottles of lager paid for each one of you in the NAAFI canteen this afternoon.''

''Thanks kindly sir, but it isn't necessary – we'd back you up whatever happened.''

''I know that killick, but this is a sort of present on behalf of Nuisance. That dog's over the moon with joy at his ride.''

''Then we'll drink Nuisance's health, as well as yours sir.''

The pilot caught the van back to the officers quarters and reported to the flight commander, filled in his patrol report and placed it in the daily flight record, then went off for a welcome shower and meal.

After lunch I changed into swimming trunks and, grabbing a towel, walked to the open-air swimming pool. There, about a dozen others and three Wrens were swimming or sunning themselves on the concrete surround. I saw to my surprise that Nuisance was dog-paddling down the stretch of water. He reached the far end, rested his forepaws on the concrete and heaved himself out. Seeing me, he bounded up and licked my hand before running off towards the NAAFI and his midday quart of lager.

A few days later I met Nuisance again and was in time to see what actually happened. I was standing in front of a block about 5 o'clock in the evening waiting for our three-ton lorry to arrive to take us to town.

The lorry was rounding the sharp bend leading from the main base road to the entrance to the block. About two dozen yards from us, as the vehicle started to brake, we saw Nuisance take a flying leap from the back of the lorry over the tailboard and land awkwardly on the tarmac. As he fell, one of his hind legs skidded to one side and his nose scraped along the ground.

Several of us ran over to him and he was trying to rise on all fours, but couldn't manage. The lorry driver, an able seaman, was telling us that he'd picked up Nuisance at the guardroom, helped him up over the tailboard and assumed that the dog was heading for the ratings' billets or the canteen. A pilot, who had been studying for a medical career when the war intervened, made Nuisance lie still while he examined him. I held his head and he licked my hand. The dog never made a sound as the young pilot felt all round his haunches, legs, back, chest and head.

One thing I *could* see, the black pug nose had a nasty looking gash on it which was bleeding profusely. I stroked the dog's head and murmured, "Lie still Nuisance old son, we'll look after you."

He licked my hand, and a sound that was half yawn, part moan, came from his wide-open mouth. The pilot who was examining him turned and said he didn't think the dog had broken bones and we should try to lift him to his feet. Nuisance tried, but his left hind leg gave way and he sank to the ground again.

I went into the block and phoned the sick-bay.

An ambulance arrived with a lieutenant-surgeon sitting beside the driver and two male nurses carrying a stretcher emerged from the back doors. The surgeon gave Nuisance a quick examination and said they'd better get him to the X-ray department although, if he had broken a bone, it certainly wasn't a compound fracture.

They lifted him on the stretcher and put him in the back of the ambulance. Nuisance looked at me with a pleading expression on his face, and I asked the medical officer if I could help in any way, adding that the dog was friendly towards me.

A pilot suddenly said:

"Nuisance will be OK Terry, the MO reckons he's not too bad – yet you're acting as if he was your best friend."

"Perhaps he is Sub-Lieutenant Bryant or, at least, I hope he will be."

I climbed in the back of the ambulance and sat beside Nuisance stroking his head, and he licked my fingers. We arrived at the sick-bay. The two male nurses carried Nuisance into the treatment room, laid him on an examination table and the surgeon gave him a thorough check. He soon established that the trouble was high on the left hind-quarters. Whenever the MO touched that spot Nuisance raised his head and whined.

"There's no sign of visible damage, but my guess is he's torn a haunch muscle or perhaps a greenstick fracture of a bone near that spot. Anyway, as you know, we have no X-ray equipment here. We'll have to get him to the Royal Navy Hospital at Simon's Town and they have excellent facilities if an operation is required.

"My two male nurses will ride in the ambulance with him, as the important thing is to make him lie still."

About an hour later we arrived at Simon's Town Naval Hospital and the attendants carried Nuisance inside. Two nursing sisters admitted him and put him in a bed in a side ward and then a surgeon-commander appeared who looked first at Nuisance and then at me, read a note one of the male nurses handed to him, written by the surgeon-lieutenant at Wingfield.

The surgeon gestured to Nuisance who raised his head, yawned and licked the doctor's hand. After that things happened quickly. I was put in a waiting room, given a cup of tea by a pretty young nurse while Nuisance was put on a hospital trolley and led to the X-ray department.

An hour later the commander appeared in the waiting-room. He held two or three X-ray films in his hand, and waving them at me remarked, "Rest easy, Nuisance has no broken bones, just a badly-torn muscle. I'll attend to that in the morning – he'll be good as new in about seven days. You can see him for a few minutes if you like, but I've given him an injection to relieve the pain and help him sleep. Tell me, why are you especially interested in him?"

I explained about having a young Great Dane puppy at home and the commander smiled.

"Well that clears up the answer to that question. But it still doesn't explain why he seems so fond of you."

"I've been trying to make friends with him for a good number of weeks now sir, done one or two favours for him and he's just started to act a bit friendly."

"Been arranging rides for him, have you?" asked the surgeon.

I felt my face redden. How had the doctor guessed Nuisance had been on a flight? The surgeon must have noticed my reaction to his question and murmured, "Only meant a lift into Cape Town, but I think there's a little more to it than that, isn't there? Still it's best if I don't press the question, the less I know the better, eh?"

He led me into a small ward which had three beds in it. Nuisance was in the middle one with a rating on each side of him in the other two beds. He was lying with his head on the pillow and a nurse was giving, or trying to give him, a spoonful of medicine. Nuisance, although his eyes were half-closed, kept jerking his head away whenever the spoon was near his huge jaws.

I gently led the nurse to one side and took the spoon from her hand saying, "I apologise on his behalf nurse, but I'm afraid Nuisance doesn't care much for ladies, except those of his own breed. I'll give him his medicine.''

I approached Nuisance who was now yawning continuously, obviously the injection was taking effect. I stroked his head and held out the spoonful of medicine and said to him,

"Come on Nuisance, have a sip of lager old lad.''

At the word lager his ears shot upright, I could see his tail wagging beneath the bed-clothes, but he raised his head and let me pour the medicine down his throat, gulped, but swallowed it and his drowsy eyes glared at me in reproach for having tricked him. To make amends I said, "It was for your own good Nuisance – and get better quickly, then we'll arrange another trip up there,'' and pointed to the ceiling motioning with my hands as if they were outstretched wings.

His glazing eyes brightened for a moment and he lifted one paw off the pillow, then lay down and started to snore. Whether he understood what I'd just promised I'll never know but there was no doubt that he had dropped off into a deep, painless sleep.

I said good-bye to the nurse and on my way down the corridor saw the surgeon commander and told him of Nuisance's aversion to women, that it would be better for all concerned if Nuisance was looked after by a male nurse, and could I ring each day to find out how Nuisance was?

The commander grinned and handed me a card saying,

"There's my telephone number on this card. Ring any time between nine in the morning and six at night and I'll give you the latest gen. As to male nurses, I know Nuisance's likes and dislikes, that's been taken care of. Now get off into town and relax. Nuisance will be fine in a few days, he'll get the best care possible. Remember, I like that dog just as much as you do.''

The commander, in spite of the difference in our ranks, gripped my hand and gave me a firm handshake, saying as a final parting:

"Take care, remember the posters about 'Careless talk costs lives.'

After his fifth day in hospital the commander told me Nuisance had been allowed out of bed and, although he still had a slight limp in his left hind leg, another three or four days' rest would cure that. However, it would be some time before the injury was fully healed and he could gallop about at his own speed. I asked the commander if he would let me know when Nuisance was discharged from hospital and if it would be alright to fetch him back to Wingfield in a jeep.

The surgeon-commander asked: "You've a very fine open-air swimming pool at Wingfield, haven't you, Sisson?''

"Yes sir, and Nuisance enjoys a swim in it whenever he is on the aerodrome, but is there any reason for asking?''

"There is – get Nuisance in there every day if he returns to Wingfield. Make him swim three or four lengths of the pool every day, it's the finest therapeutic treatment I know, is swimming, for curing injured muscles and limbs.''

Came the day the commander phoned and said I could fetch Nuisance if he would accompany me. I raised the question about what if he wanted to stay in the pool for quite a long while?

The Commander was adamant, no more than five minutes for the first few days, then longer as time passed.

I borrowed a jeep from Wingfield's transport section and set off for Simon's Town. When I arrived at the steps of the hospital I saw two Great Danes at the top, Nuisance and his brother Bats. But a rating was holding each dog and, instead of fighting, they were licking each other's faces. When I saw Nuisance towering above Bats I realised for the first time just how massive he really was, and how much broader across the shoulders.

As the rating led Nuisance down the steps and he saw me sitting in the jeep I patted the seat beside me and called:

"Come on Nuisance, there's a quart of lager waiting for you at Wingfield."

At the word lager his floppy ears pricked and his jaws slavered then, probably remembering what I'd given him to drink last time I'd spoken that word, he looked me full in the face and gave another ear-shattering bark of disbelief.

Just then a group of ratings in square rig walked by and Nuisance made as if to join them. So I stepped quickly out of the jeep and pointing up to the sky shouted,

"How about a trip up there Nuisance?"

He stopped, lifted a forepaw and, as he looked up into the blue sky which I had indicated with my hand, I noticed that the gash on his nose was practically healed.

Then his gaze swung back to me. He glanced skywards again and his recollection of the Albacore flight gained his full support. He trotted forward and I opened the jeep door and helped him on the passenger seat. Sitting on his haunches he peered all round and levelled his gaze on the ratings who had stopped to stare at their oppo. The expressions on their faces plainly showed their disapproval. Nuisance's nose went up and he sat beside me as if he wished to show he was king of all he surveyed. His tongue flicked across my face and it was as if a piece of pumice stone had rasped my cheek.

I started the engine but, just as I was about to drive off, the surgeon-commander came running down the steps. He held out his hand to Nuisance who responded at once. His paw shot out for a shake. After all here was a man who had cured him twice now and, officer or not, in Nuisance's mind this placed him firmly in the same category as his rating oppos.

"Is it all right for Nuisance to have a quart of lager and a good meal when we get back to Wingfield sir?"

The commander laughed.

"Let him have two or three quarts, if he wants. And as much meat as he can eat will help him get his strength back. I've seen to it that he's

An Albacore aircraft of the Fleet Air Arm, of the type in which Just Nuisance kept "dog-watches" on aerial patrols along the Cape coast.

had at least two quarts of lager every day, so thank God my pocket will no longer be subject to free drinks every day. And, one last little warning. Be very careful, for your own sake, about those trips with Nuisance."

"I will sir, and thanks very much for all you've done."

I drove back to Wingfield and made straight for one of the hangars where a leading air mechanic was working, and asked him if he'd put Nuisance up in his billet for three or four days. The LAM was delighted, and I asked him to bring Nuisance to the swimming pool about five each evening, and that this was according to doctor's orders.

As I opened the jeep door for Nuisance to climb out he trotted straight into the hangar, stalked to the aircraft and walked all round it. Then he came back, gripped my cuff sleeve in his mouth and pulled me towards the plane.

The four maintenance men were grinning and the LAM remarked, "He's ready for another patrol."

"I'm afraid that'll have to be postponed for a while, even the surgeon at Simon's Town hospital has a good idea Nuisance isn't a stranger to the clouds. But I'm not taking any chances LAM; we'll wait a few weeks before he enjoys another trip."

The next evening at five the air mechanic delivered Nuisance to me at the swimming pool. I dived in at one end and, surfacing, shouted for Nuisance to follow. The dog trotted back from the edge of the pool, turned, took a short run and made his usual wild plunge into the water.

His style was to leap out as far as possible, all four legs wide-spread, so that his stomach hit the water in a smacking belly-flop. The great spout of water was as if a miniature depth charge had been dropped.

At the same time he let out one great bark of sheer pleasure.

After paddling up the pool, his huge forepaws creating small tidal waves, he climbed out on the concrete surround. This time I was waiting for him and turned him round to swim back. He looked at me in surprise, but I pointed to the sky and his eyes lit up in recognition. As I swam in a swift free-style stroke back down the stretch of pool Nuisance followed me. Climbing out, I waited for his paws to grip the concrete and hauled him out. This procedure went on for five evenings and, at the end of that time, all signs of lameness had gone.

Out and About

By the end of August 1943, Nuisance had become my regular companion both in trips to Cape Town and at the sea-side resorts round the Peninsula such as Sea Point, Muizenberg, and the half a dozen other beautiful beaches within a short train ride.

Several other incidents occurred on the trains on our way to these pleasure spots.

By now 99 per cent of travellers on the suburban trains knew the dog by sight (and sound), but there were the unfortunate one per cent that didn't.

The first untoward event occurred when Nuisance and I, having spent a wonderful afternoon at Muizenberg, had made friends with a bunch of young children playing on the beach with a large plastic ball. Finally, one of them threw it and hit his nose.

Nuisance was furious – after all, his nose was the most tender part of his anatomy, besides being of great service in determining whether a meal would be tasty or the lager was the right brand . . .

He pounced on the ball. His huge mouth practically encircled it as his paws ripped at it. A few seconds later it burst with a loud bang. Nuisance leapt high off the sand with shock. However, he was quickly sorry that he'd spoiled his young pals' fun. He took the remains of the ball in his mouth and walked over, dropped it on the sand, cocked his head on one side and held out his paw in apology.

As I chided him Nuisance looked at me with sorrowful eyes, fully realising he had committed some form of bad manners.

It was nearly four months since Nuisance's last flight and I had promised him, in obvious gestures by pointing to the sky, that I would soon organise a repeat of the biggest thrill of his life. In some uncanny way he knew the time was rapidly approaching. Often when we were out walking together he'd stop, sit on his haunches in a begging posture and keep glancing at the sky. I had to laugh at this obvious request for another trip into the wild blue yonder.

As we stood on the station platform at Muizenberg for a train to Cape Town, there were several ratings who knew him.

The train arrived and, as usual, Nuisance was first to board. The coach was pretty full already but all the ratings found seats, and I was lucky to find one vacant between two middle-aged women. Nuisance still hadn't found his customary two adjoining seats where he could spread himself in comfort. Opposite me was a young woman sitting near the window, dressed in the khaki uniform of the South African Women's Auxiliary.·

From the badges, she was in the artillery branch.

She looked demure and, from the glances she kept directing at Nuisance, did not know who he was. Probably it was the first time she'd ever seen the canine AB – and there was an empty seat next to her.

Nuisance suddenly walked towards her, but I did not guess his intention in time to avoid what happened. He leapt on the empty seat, placed both forepaws against her shoulders and pushed her off into the aisle. The ratings seated neaby reached the girl before I could and an able seaman helped her up and said:

"Don't be scared of him miss. It's only Nuisance; he doesn't like ladies, whether they're in uniform or not; he's a sailor's dog, but he would do exactly the same thing if a lady was dressed in Wrens uniform. He thinks that every seat on the train belongs to him when he's on board. Sit in my seat miss."

She did so and was soon chatting to several of the ratings, while Nuisance had now stretched full-length with his fore-legs crossed over his eyes to shut out the light.

I did not intend this rudeness by Nuisance to go unpunished, so as the train stopped at the next station and one of the women seated near me left the train, I walked over to Nuisance, seated myself on the end of his seat and pushed his hindquarters forward. Without taking his paws from his eyes, he shoved both his hind legs violently against my thighs – no doubt thinking it was the young girl trying to regain her seat.

I, too, finished up in the aisle and the ratings tittered. So did the army girl. I grinned at them and then spoke loudly to Nuisance:

"Nuisance, no lager for you tonight and no meat pies – not because you knocked me on the floor but for what you did to the young lady."

I was standing in the aisle as I spoke and Nuisance at once jumped off his seat and, hanging his head down with his tail tucked disconsolately between his legs, must have realised who he'd kicked. He licked my hand, sat up in his usual begging position and held out one paw in abject apology. The pleading look forced me to take his paw and shake it. He was ecstatic, jumped back to his seat, sat up straight and kept patting the space next to him for me to sit down. This was indeed an honour – one of his paws inviting me to take a seat next to him.

I crossed over to the girl and introduced myself. She told me her name was Miss Jill Martin and she was stationed near Cape Town. I apologised for Nuisance's behaviour; she graciously accepted the apology. (This young woman now lives in East London and her account of the incident appeared in the *Daily Dispatch*, on May 28, 1984.)

Next morning I had a word with the LAM regarding Nuisance's next flight and we decided to have him on board in two days' time. When I suggested that the LAM let Nuisance sleep in his billet for the next two nights he asked me:

"You've never had Nuisance in your quarters all night, have you?"

"No, but I'm working on plans to do that. Just an odd night now and

117

then. What made you ask?''

"Well, he's been in my billet two dozen times or more during the past year, or in one of the billets near mine, and us chaps talk together about him and some of the funny habits he has when asleep. Quite comical, some of them. Wouldn't believe it, unless you actually see them yourself.''

I was very curious.

"Well, you know how he sleeps in bed, head on the pillow just like his oppos and his front paws dangling over the edge. There's always one dim lamp alight in the billets at night so ratings can go outside to the 'heads'. That lets us see him asleep.

"Well, sometimes he'll lift his head right off the pillow, and snap at the empty air – the next second he's fast asleep. Then many's the time I've heard him actually laughing in his sleep, a sort of chuckling noise as if he's having a nice dream. It's amazing how close it sounds to a rating laughing when he's awake. In fact, a chap out of a billet near mine swears he got on to the rating in the next bed to Nuisance – thought it was him laughing – and told the bloke, if he wanted to laugh in the middle of the night, to go outside. Just as they started to argue Nuisance laughed in his sleep again.

"Soon there was a group of them standing round Nuisance's bed watching him laugh. Lasted for about 20 minutes, Nuisance laughing I mean. Then he turned over in bed and there wasn't another giggle from him for the rest of the night.''

The LAM claimed that this happened quite often, perhaps two or three times a week, sometimes he laughed only for a minute or two then, as soon as he moved in bed, the sound would stop.

Three days later, in the company of an oppo from my squadron, we caught the evening train to Cape Town. Having a drink in the Grand Hotel, we got talking to two members of the South African Women's Auxiliary Army Service. My chum and his acquaintance opted to go to the Alhambra cinema while my newly-met girlfriend and I walked up Adderley Street to the Texas Bar (Standard Hotel) for more liquid refreshment.

As I looked up at the hotel's balcony I saw Nuisance with his paws on the rail, contemplating Adderley Street below. He didn't see me. I went to the bar and spoke to the manager who knew me well by now. As I ordered our drinks I asked the manager to take out Nuisance's chamber pot and pour a quart of lager in it. My girlfriend, whose name was Joyce, giggled when she saw me carrying the pot, plus two meat pies I'd bought at the bar, and making for the stairs to the balcony. As we reached the upper floor I chose the nearest table to the stairs and, for once, there were no other customers present.

Joyce gripped my arm and murmured as we sat down. "Look Terry, there's Nuisance leaning on the rails.'' Telling her to stay where she was, I laid the pot of lager down, put the two meat pies beside it and, in a quiet voice, called out to him:

"Nuisance, come on boy, big eats.''

At the sound of my voice his front paws hit the floor with a thump and he bounded towards me. I knelt down and stroked his floppy ears while he put one front paw on my thigh, and his great sandpaper-like tongue licked my face. There was no doubt he was pleased. He pranced around and his tail wagged in a swift blur. Then I indicated the lager and pies. He looked me in the eyes and held out his paw. I shook it, and his great black snout dived into the pot. After half-emptying it, he started on the pies. His table manners were impeccable as ever. First he placed one paw on top of the crust and with his other front paw he deftly removed all the pastry, leaving this unwanted human-type flavouring for any would-be scavengers, and gulped down the meat.

Then he took another few swigs at his favourite brew and started on the second pie – meat only, of course.

Joyce whispered excitedly, "Why, that dog adores you Terry!"

Nuisance trotted up to my table and ignoring Joyce, placed his head in my lap while I fondled his ears and murmured softly, "Get back to Wingfield Nuisance, and we'll arrange another trip." I pointed my fingers to the sky and, as I have said before, the dog could not understand my words but something in my voice and perhaps my gesture was enough for him to grasp what I was trying to convey.

He started whirling round my table, trying to bite his tail, for a minute or two. Much later that night I wondered if my words had raised his morale to a higher pitch than it usually was.

Finally he calmed down and held out his paw again. Joyce tried to stroke his head and he seemed to notice her for the first time. He ducked away from her hand, a menacing rumble sounded and the girl shrank in alarm. He looked me in the eyes once more and, it may have been my imagination, but I had a distinct impression he objected to my being with a young girl. Then he raised his head, gave one gruff bark and bounded off down the stairs.

Later that night Joyce and I entered the City Hall, as there was a concert on. The show was half over by the time we took our seats in the second row from the front and, as we sat down, I saw Nuisance stretch out in the aisle just below the stage. Whether he had seen me go into the building and followed, or whether it was pure coincidence, I shall never know but am inclined to believe it was the former possibility.

The band was playing and there was a contralto singing. She was a middle-aged woman and had a fine voice. Her dress was of sequins and frothy lace which swirled about when she moved. The tune was an aria not much to Nuisance's taste.

I knew that the dog attended the City Hall in Cape Town quite often but, not yet having heard about him invading the stage two years before in chase of an imaginary rat, didn't realize there might be trouble. I was wrong.

I laughed and, tapping Joyce's arm, pointed at Nuisance. He was lying flat out in the aisle and had both forepaws pressed across each ear. Joyce giggled and whispered.

"They ought to play God Save the King. I've seen him in the drill hall near here at a dance, and I swear he barks in tune to it, stands strictly at attention too, tail pointing straight up in the air," she giggled again. I saw Nuisance turn his head and I think he saw me. I waved my hand and he suddenly leapt on the stage. The large-bosomed contralto took one glance at Nuisance's massive frame and promptly fainted.

Three or four ratings jumped on the platform and led Nuisance away.

A nurse from the audience was holding a bottle of smelling salts to the singer's nose and soon had her up once more. Clasping her forehead, she staggered to the wings. The manager appeared and seemed to be intent on evicting Nuisance who had calmly resumed his former position in the centre of the aisle. However, there were so many protests from ratings present that he gave up in disgust and waved the next act on.

It was an unfortunate choice in view of what happened.

A juggler came on dressed as a clown. First he twirled Indian clubs, then he changed to dishes, and I noticed Nuisance watching the whirling objects with fascination, his head darting about trying to focus on each article. His ears were up and his tail swished across the floor. (Perhaps the plates reminded him of grub).

Then the fatal mistake . . . .

The juggler briefly went to the wings and came out holding a Pomeranian dog on a silken leash. He held a gaudy ball in his other hand which he placed on the tiny dog's nose. The pooch balanced it, then flipped it up into the juggler's hand.

I got up and moved towards Nuisance. But I was too late, and so were five square-rigged ratings – or perhaps I should say Nuisance was too fast for us. He had been offended in two ways. Firstly, it was his prerogative to be the only animal around naval ratings. Secondly, one of their favourite games when they played was to throw a ball for him to retrieve. I'd seen him do this many times. That, too, was his prerogative, and the goings-on across the footlights constituted a double threat to his jurisdiction.

He gave an ear-splitting bark and leapt. The pom must have thought an athletic elephant had been allowed in the audience. It disappeared beneath the draped curtains that hung in the wings. The juggler also ran but the coloured ball proved a life-saving distraction. Nuisance caught it as it rolled over the stage, chomped and shook his head. It wasn't a ball any longer, as it fell, just a flattened piece of rubber.

By this time the five sailors and myself were on the stage and trying to hold Nuisance. The audience, especially the women, were running out of the doors, and a lot of servicemen weren't far behind them. I managed to get a grip on Nuisance's neck and, though he growled, he recognised me and calmed down a bit. Finally I was able to lead him down just as the manager, flanked by five men of the naval patrol, came inside.

The petty officer in charge approached and clasped his head in his hands, crying out: "Bloody hell! Not Nuisance again, for God's sake. I should let that dog go if I was you. He's more trouble than a dozen ratings put together.

"Is he in your charge?"

"Nuisance is never in anybody's charge, you should know that. He was behaving himself till a juggler brought another dog on the stage – and that's like waving a red flag at a bull."

The PO wiped his forehead with a handkerchief, and asked, "Was anyone injured?". I thought it prudent not to mention the singer fainting and replied, "Just a storm in a tea cup PO.

"Alright, seeing no one's been injured, just let's get the hall cleared."

I had a word with one of the sailors outside and asked him to put Nuisance on the train to Wingfield. He promised to do so, but then said: "Us lads won't forget you; what you done for Nuisance I mean. Isn't one of us, or even half a dozen of us, who could have quietened him like you did."

I joined Joyce at the door of the City Hall. She looked a bit pale so I took her to a hotel for a drink. Her colour returned and she gazed at me as if I was some kind of hero. "That was a very brave thing you did Terry, grabbing Nuisance like that; he's so strong and powerful; weren't you afraid?"

I laughed and told a white lie.

"Not for a moment Joyce, that dog's my friend. He wouldn't harm me." I didn't let on that I'd been frightened enough, when I gripped Nuisance round the neck and felt the awesome power the dog had in his huge frame.

Just after dawn the following day, our Albacore pilot was picked up by the aircrew van at the officers' quarters, dressed in flying kit and carrying helmet and goggles. The TAG was already aboard and, five minutes later, we stood outside the hangar waiting while the labourers shoved the aircraft outside.

The LAM came dashing up, excitement on his face, and whispered: "Nuisance came back to my billet last night, sir. He's already tied down in the observer's seat. He's pretty excited – I should let your TAG keep a firm hold on him till you're airborne. Nobody knows but me and the other three maintenance crew."

The pilot replied: "Thanks LAM, we'll be careful. Have everything laid on for getting him out when we return."

He climbed into the pilot's seat and the TAG settled himself in the rear part of the cockpit. Nuisance was stretched out on the floor, tied by his collar to the angle iron of a seat-anchoring cleat.

His tail was swishing and his whole frame was quivering with expectation.

The pilot plugged in his intercom and R/T set, contacted the control tower and asked permission for take-off. The "affirmative" reply followed and, noting the direction of the wind from the windsock, he turned into the breeze and opened the throttle.

Three minutes later the Albacore was airborne and, after making a single circuit of the 'drome, set course for the coast and the waters of the South Atlantic. After passing over the beach near Fish Hoek the TAG released Nuisance. Like a flash he was on his hind legs, front paws resting on the perspex canopy and peering down towards the sea, which was calm except for the odd rolling Atlantic swell.

The pilot could feel Nuisance's tongue licking the back of his helmet and, even though the intercom headphones were clamped to his ears, could still pick up his intermittent barks of pleasure. Suddenly the intercom buzzer sounded and the TAG reported:

"Look at Nuisance skipper. He's spotted something; keeps jumping up and down and looking towards the sea on our port quarter." The pilot dropped lower and swung the aircraft in the direction Nuisance was watching so intently.

Then he saw why Nuisance was so excited.

A school of dolphins or porpoises were leaping from the surface of the sea and the Albacore circled round them. Nuisance nearly went wild. Whether he thought they were canine oppos or potential enemies below, swimming in the waves, I'm not sure but he was barking enthusiastically, his head swinging sideways, downwards and towards the pilot, who let him enjoy himself watching the aquatic mammals for a while then climbed back to 5000 feet. The bombs and depth charges carried were for bigger fish than this – U-boats that had surfaced to re-charge their batteries. We always received detailed reports at our dawn briefing about what convoys were in our patrol areas and also information regarding Allied submarines. One of the squadron two months before while on patrol had spotted a U-boat and dropped his anti-submarine charges. He reported that he had not sunk the enemy submarine but was sure he had damaged it. I never saw a single enemy sub during patrols but, simply because of our presence in the skies, this would prevent submerged U-boats from surfacing.

After about a two-hour flight, with Nuisance never taking his eyes off the water below except for an occasional glance at the white clouds overhead, the TAG spoke over the intercom.

"Skipper, three or four miles on the starboard wing, about 2 o'clock, large fast liner. Looks like that troop-carrier the *Nieuw Amsterdam* we were briefed about is heading for the Cape."

"I see it TAG. We'll climb a bit and circle for a half hour or so to see if any U-boat is tracking it – but he won't have much chance as she's doing nearly 30 knots, that's why it's not necessary for her to be in convoy. We'll flash a message by Aldis when we are overhead."

The pilot set course for the liner and Nuisance spotted the ship and commenced to rear up on his hind legs so he could get a better view. He started barking again with his tail thumping the leather-covered back of the observer's seat.

"TAG, tie down Nuisance. I'm about to make a pass over the liner and, ten to one, there's a senior Royal Navy officer aboard. I'm taking no more chances".

"OK skipper," he replied.

The TAG was having a hell of a job trying to get Nuisance down from his perch, so the pilot reached over behind, patted the dog on his head and pointed to the floor of the aircraft. He seemed to understand and dropped down to all fours, but reluctantly. The TAG tied him down.

Two and a half hours later as the Albacore taxied up to the hangar a swarm of labourers came rushing out. Nuisance had been released after the plane left the liner astern, resuming his watching brief at the side screen and tied down again just before the coast was crossed.

The aircraft was wheeled inside the hangar and the pilot followed. His four loyal mechanics were waiting inside and, as the aircraft was parked in its designated spot, the labourers were waved outside. Nuisance was lifted down from the cockpit. As soon as his feet touched the concrete he ran to the front landing wheels, then to the rear one, sniffing the tyres. Next he raced round the hangar, black nose lifted in ecstasy, bounding in the air and again trying to bite his own tail. Suddenly, to my horror, I saw the commander (flying) enter the hangar, noticing his car parked near the door.

Nuisance trotted over to me, placed his paws on my shoulders and his leathery tongue licked my face. Pushing him down I turned to face the flying commander, who halted just in front of me and said,

"What's Nuisance doing in here?

"Nuisance is very chummy with the LAM, sir. Sleeps in his billet most nights; goes to meals with him and to the canteen. Have you any objection to his presence in here sir?"

The commander was, as I knew just as fond of Nuisance as our CO and he replied:

"Not at all, except that I'd like you to warn the mechanics not to test the engine while he's in here. The dog could walk into the propeller."

The Commander strode to his car.

I wiped the sweat from my brow. If he had arrived five minutes sooner he'd have seen Nuisance being lifted from the cockpit and, much as he would hate doing it, a report of a flagrant breach of regulations would have been forwarded to the CO. He, in turn, would have had no option but to pass it on to the C-in-C for a possible court-martial.

I reflected that twice Nuisance had placed us in a position where we could have been in serious trouble. The affair at the City Hall, and to-day's flight. Still, I mused, Nuisance was not human. He could no more hide his feelings than the pilot could fly without his aircraft. When he was displeased he plainly showed it; when excited and happy he also made that clear. As if to prove the latter point, he now jumped up on my shoulders again and flicked his tongue over my chin. Then, to my amazement, he walked all round the aircraft, stroking a paw over the landing gear. Rearing up on his hind legs, he started to lick the tail-plane.

Nuisance then walked over and took the cuff of my jacket in his mouth, pulling me towards the van. I climbed in beside the TAG and Nuisance jumped inside and sprawled at my feet still quivering with joy. He placed one paw on my boot as if daring me to move away from him. I was thirsty, so shouted to the driver to make for the canteen.

The canteen hadn't opened yet but apparently the TAG was friendly with the manageress and, as we alighted from the van, he disappeared round the back of the building. Nuisance and I followed.

The Albacore crew knocked on the door which was quickly opened by the woman in charge who looked around outside for a second or two, then beckoned them through.

Nuisance led the way and as he negotiated the several corners of the passageway it was plain that he knew the direction of the bar. The pilot explained that he had just landed from a flight and that couldn't obtain a drink at the officers' quarters. The manageress nodded sympathetically, poured a pint of lager each and then a quart for Nuisance in a big bowl. He downed this before we were half done, and had finished another quart by the time we'd drained our beer.

The dog was still trembling a little with excitement. He leapt on one of the settees and, to our amusement, lifted a paw, raised his head towards the ceiling, then looked down at the floor, parodying his movements while on the flight!

As I prepared to leave Nuisance began to follow, but I took him back to the TAG and asked him to take him over. "Stay here Nuisance; I'll see you again soon – and behave yourself, mind."

Of course, he couldn't understand what I'd said. But again the tone of my voice must have reassured him that I wasn't angry. He licked my hand, pranced round a step or two and his tail started wagging again.

The Angry Commodore

Some weeks later I had arranged to meet Joyce at seven near the City Hall, so walked down Adderley Street with Nuisance padding along contentedly by my side. When I reached the City Hall Joyce was waiting but Nuisance, on seeing me greet her, backed off and his head started swinging round as if seeking escape. Joyce tried to stroke him but the dog would have none of this and stared at me with accusing eyes.

Why spoil an oppo's night out in town by dragging a female along, his face seemed to say. I thought the best thing to do, if he was in this mood, was to leave him in the company of some ratings. So we headed for The Good Cheer Club where I knew there was a dance most evenings, and free food and cigarettes for servicemen, provided by the kindly citizens of Cape Town.

As Joyce walked beside me, her arm linked in mine, Nuisance trailed behind, tail dragging between his hind legs and nose close to the ground, a sure sign of ill-humour.

I did not feel as if I'd let him down in any way, as many times I had accompanied him on the train to Cape Town and, even before I'd alighted, he had bounded out of the station to meet his beloved oppos. But tonight, somehow, he'd sensed it was no ordinary evening and had expected something special.

We went into The Good Cheer Club, where a band was playing a waltz and a committee member welcomed Joyce and I. Then, seeing Nuisance trailing behind, smiled delightedly and tried to stroke him, but he edged away. Several couples were dancing to the music, most of the men being naval ratings, and Nuisance wandered on to the dance floor and promptly lay down in the middle of it.

Two or three ratings tried to move him, but he was determined to display his bad temper and angrily shoved them away, either with his head or paws. I tried to move him myself but he looked at me as if I was a complete stranger, so I gave up the attempt.

We stayed about half an hour and Nuisance's manner changed suddenly. He reared up, placed his fore paws on a startled rating's shoulders and began moving round the dance floor in time to a slow fox trot.

I motioned to Joyce that we should leave now that Nuisance was in the company of other oppos and I had no doubts that he would enjoy himself from now on.

There was no coastal patrol the next morning so I gathered up my swimming trunks and a towel, as during the past few weeks I had developed a habit of taking a dip in the open-air pool. Without wishing to blow my own trumpet, I had never yet met any man on the base who could match me for speed in free-style swimming, or anyone else who could swim two lengths of the pool underwater as I could . . . .

Usually at that time in the morning a light, clammy mist hung like an aura over the whole aerodrome and it wasn't till the sun broke through about nine that one could discern the looming mass of Table Mountain from Wingfield. Sometimes there would be a thin film of ice on the pool's surface that early in the morning and I usually swam only two lengths, one of them underwater, dried myself off and hurried back to my quarters about three hundred metres away for my breakfast.

As I opened the outer door, however, I nearly fell over Nuisance who was lying there waiting. He'd forgiven me for deserting him the previous night and showed it by leaping up and licking my face, then followed me down to the pool. Nuisance himself liked a swim and on his service documents there was this listing as to a man's (or Wren's) swimming abilities. Nuisance's swimming instructor had put the letters VG (very good) in this column — but it was fortunate that diving techniques did not have to be shown.

When Nuisance and I reached the pool it was deserted, and I made a racing dive and set off at a fast crawl stroke to the far end. The water was very cold with a faint, icy sheen on top. As I reached the other side I heard Nuisance's loud belly smack as he, too, plunged in, and laughed at his antics. It was evident that he'd never taken to the pool when it was so cold. Instead of swimming for the far end, he propelled himself as fast as possible to the near side, his breath rasping like that of a human with a severe bout of asthma. He heaved himself out on to the concrete surround, shook his body so vigorously that droplets of water reached the opposite side of the pool. I swam back to where Nuisance stood, still shaking his body, and could plainly hear his teeth chattering. His tail stood up starkly like a ship's mast, then he started running round the pool to raise his body temperature.

I dived in again and, leaning my arms on the edge, shouted. "Come on Nuisance, just one more dip then I'll take you to the dining hall for big eats."

Hearing the last two words, which he understood very well, he stopped racing about and as I motioned towards the water he advanced with a good deal of caution to the edge, lowered one paw to test the surface, withdrew it again as if he'd touched a hot coal, shook his head, stared at me as if I was crazy and raced off, disappearing towards the ratings' dining hall. Big eats he would enjoy. Diving into the icy water, even at my request, was in his opinion stupid. Once was enough, twice would rob him of his appetite.

I didn't see him for two days, but heard from our LAM that he was roaming round the aerodrome and had even been in the hanger twice, touching the undercarriage of our aircraft with his front paws, then rearing up on the tail-plane to lick the metal surface.

During the third day after our morning dip in the pool it was a hot, sunny afternoon. In swimming trunks I started towards the pool. Crossing the sandy soil I could hear voices and laughter, which meant there would be a crowd of officers and ratings enjoying themselves. Suddenly Nuisance appeared by my side.

I stopped and fondled his ears and he shoved his damp black nose against my thigh, rumbling with enjoyment and content. Suddenly he stopped and stared at the ground ahead, moved his body in front of my legs, forcing me to stop. He crept cautiously forward, halted, lifted up one paw, glanced back at me to ensure I wasn't moving then crept on his belly forward once more. Then he started running in a circle round something on the sandy soil, but he didn't bark or utter any sound.

His tail was wagging, but only in short arcs.

I walked forward slowly and then saw the object of his attention. A large scorpion was itself moving in an elliptical circuit inside the area Nuisance was circling. He saw me approaching and raced back to me, making me stop again. Then he shot back to his patrol duties. The scorpion kept turning its body to keep Nuisance in sight. Its tail with the venomous sting at the tip arching over the scaly back with convulsive regularity.

I remembered our surgeon's lectures on poisonous bites either by scorpions or snakes. Providing a person wasn't stung near the throat or head, the bites rarely proved fatal — especially if medical attention was available soon after being bitten. Three or four men on the aerodrome over the past two years had been bitten but, after two or three days in hospital, all had completely recovered. But bites did leave a large swelling and were painful for a day or two. Young babies, however, had no resistance in their blood to such venom and, if stung or bitten, some of them might die.

Nuisance kept circling his prey, gradually narrowing the perimeter. The scorpion, as if hypnotised by his movements, was now turning only within the length of its body. Immediately Nuisance closed in. Lifting one leg, he directed a jet of urine directly at the creature's body. It could have been the uric acid or the sudden deluge that had enveloped it, but the scorpion curled up with its tail lying motionless across the lobster-like body.

To my amazement Nuisance turned his hindquarters to the scorpion and his rear legs lashed out so quickly that all I saw was a blur of movement. The creature flew high in the air and seemed, during its flight, to come apart in two pieces. They landed metres away.

Now Nuisance let out his shattering bark and trotted towards the spot where the fragments had landed. I followed him and he stopped pawing at the ground. I looked and saw it was the tail still twitching. Nuisance put one great paw pad on it, careful not to touch the sting, pressed it deep into the sand and raked a small mound over it.

Then, his nose to the ground, he moved to his right, stopped again and waited till I came near him. He was flipping the scorpion's shell-like body which was bent into a zig-zag. This, too, was still writhing. He wasn't

so careful with this part of the body but reared on his hind-legs and brought both fore-paws down on it with such force that I heard the remnant go pop!

I knelt down and placed an arm about Nuisance's neck in a feeling of wonder and affection. But for him, some rating or officer on his way to the pool could have suffered a scorpion's sting — quite possibly me . . . .

A moment later I wished I'd not hugged him so tightly; his tongue rasped across my neck rough as a file used by one of our artificers. Let no one doubt that Nuisance knew that he had performed his good deed for the day. He curvetted in front of me, lifting up his front paws in a prancing motion that reminded me of films I'd seen of a knight's war-charger moving in to battle.

When I got to the pool it was crowded, sunbathers lying round the concrete slabs and about 40 others swimming. Nuisance lay down near our LAM who was stretched out near one corner. As it happened the senior medical officer was sitting chatting to a pilot of my squadron and I went and sat by him. He looked at my face and must have seen how excited I was and asked:

"Well, come to show off your speed doing the crawl-stroke, or how far you can swim under water, to us novices?"

"No sir, just to tell you I've just watched Nuisance do the most incredible thing I've ever seen."

"Nothing that dog does would surprise me."

I explained what Nuisance had done to the scorpion and the surgeon's eyes wandered over to where the dog was lying. "Well I'll be damned, must have been quite an event to watch, sure you're not exaggerating, just a bit?''

I felt a little angry, but he went on.

''Calm down, I once heard a similar story from a rating who was in the sick-bay for a couple of days about six months ago, I didn't know whether to believe him or not, but I do now. I know you, and I know quite a bit about Nuisance. It's exactly what I'd expect from that canine genius of an AB.''

The SMO then tapped me on the arm and pointed towards the massive figure of the most senior naval officer on the base. He was a commodore (engineer) only one rank below that of rear-admiral. In spite of his seniority he was theoretically under the command of our CO who was a captain. No one seemed to know what his duties were at the base, as he was not a Fleet Air Arm engineer but a warships' engineer. It was seldom that he appeared in the wardroom and he had spacious quarters where he ate, or dined with our CO in his special dining room. He must have been about 50, more than 1,8m in height, stout and round 17 or 18 stone (114 kg) in weight. His corpulent midriff bulged over the swimming trunks he was wearing, with a large bath towel slung round his neck.

He strode towards the pool like one of Nelson's rotund ships-of-the-line, dropped his towel and dived into the pool with a huge splash rather like Nuisance's own belly-flop.

Swimmers gave way before his big frame progressing up the pool, doing an ungainly breast stroke. When he reached the far end, puffing like a stranded whale, he climbed out with much heaving and gasping. He stood up and, as he walked by Nuisance lying by the edge of the pool, he laughed, put a flabby foot under the dog's stomach and tipped him into the water.

Nuisance disappeared under the surface, came up again and looked at the Commodore who stood on the concrete surround laughing loudly and gesturing with enjoyment at the dog's startled features. The Great Dane swam to the side and was hauled out by two of his oppos. There was an undertone of anger from ratings and officers lying round the pool at this loutish ill-treatment of Nuisance. Everyone stopped talking and laughing, and then one of the pilots, lying near me, sat up and uttered a loud ''Boo!''

This was taken up by nearly 100 ratings, officers and Wrens sunning themselves, and by swimmers in the water.

Nuisance, meanwhile, stood shaking the water from his body and kept glancing at the commodore who, after the booing had lasted about 30 seconds, drew his body up to its full height and, glaring all round him, yelled: ''Silence all of you, or I'll close the swimming pool. Can't any of you take a joke. You've all pushed some of your friends in the drink, sometime before, so what's all the moaning about — and at an officer of flag rank too?''

Someone among the crowd shouted: ''And what would you have done if one of us had shoved *you* in the pool?'' The commodore whirled round

trying to locate the man who'd shouted and, on failing to do so, walked
to where he had left his towel, stood by the edge and dived again in the
now-empty pool, with an even bigger splash than his previous effort.

He wallowed towards the far end and had the same difficulty climbing
out. I saw Nuisance trotting towards him and got hurriedly to my feet
to head the dog away from his intended victim, but I had the length of
the pool to go and hadn't a hope of averting what happened.

The commodore stood up with his back to the water, wiped his eyes
and looked in consternation at the dog who stood three yards away.
Nuisance leapt forward, his two front paws slamming into the commodore's fat belly — and I could hear the breath whoosh out of the senior
officer's lungs from where I was standing 20 metres away.

The commodore's body described a low-trajectory back dive and disappeared below the surface. Such was the force applied by Nuisance that
he, too, nearly fell in, his front paws actually touching the water. Then
he stood up on all four legs and, as the apoplectic face of the commodore
appeared, Nuisance let out one roaring bark of triumph, backed a few
steps and watched the senior officer swim to the side. Here the commodore
let out with a string of four-letter words that would have done credit to
a time-served stoker and, shaking his fist at the dog, promised the canine
AB 60 days cells on bread-and-water, expulsion from the Royal Navy with
a dishonourable discharge, and a kick up the backside when he caught
up with him.

As he clambered out of the water, to my surprise, Nuisance made off
at high speed with the commodore running after him still swearing dire
threats of revenge. This surprised me, as Nuisance was not afraid of man

or beast, and would ordinarily have stood his ground. But on reflection I realised that the dog was a wise old hand, and must have noticed how people round the pool and in the water had deferred to this human being.

To Nuisance that only meant one thing. This person wielded the same kind of authority as ticket-collectors who'd put him off trains in his younger days — so the common-sense thing to do was keep out of his way and make a trip ashore.

As Nuisance sped out of sight, there arose a loud and prolonged burst of cheering and laughter at the commodore's discomfiture and he turned his rage on us. Pointing to the group near me, as except for the SMO, they were all pilots and commissioned officers, so he knew all of them, he yelled:

"I know you lot, bloody pilots except for the sawbones, not a sodding spark of . . . discipline in any of you. Look disgraceful in uniform or out of it, bunch of . . .. I'm reporting you all to the CO and your . . . of a flying commander. And you Sisson, wipe that grin from your face, everybody knows you've got homosexual feelings for that animal, ought to be kicked out of the service and . . . will be, if I have my way.

"Now . . . off every man jack of you."

My face was burning and only with great restraint did I succeed in not attempting to punch his fat jowls. But I stood at attention and spoke quietly.

"With respect sir, I entirely reject that allegation and demand a public apology in front of our officers."

The pilots near me and the SMO all murmured agreement, but the commodore was beside himself with rage, and roared: "Not bloody likely, no apologies from me in public or in private. I gave you a bloody order just now, carry it out, and . . . off."

I could write another chapter about what transpired regarding this incident, but this is a book about Nuisance not me. Let it suffice to say that I did receive a public apology from the commodore in front of every officer on the base. Nuisance was not punished at all, and I was astounded about a week later when the commodore stopped me, pushed a large parcel in my hand and said: "Here you are, a large bone for Nuisance, and two tips from me to you. Watch out for the executive commander. He's on to your beanos (bones, lager, and rum) with Nuisance some nights. And the next time you have Nuisance taken up for a flight keep him well hidden. There's a lieutenant in the control tower who's a bit suspicious. But good luck to you my boy."

I could only stammer out:

"Thanks very much sir; it was good of you to put me on guard. I promise to use caution in future."

As I walked away I wondered how the old boy knew about my arranging trips for Nuisance in our aircraft, probably from the control tower officer, who had been tipped off by one or more of the maintenance ratings of other aircraft in our squadron. He had resolved that Nuisance's next flight would have to be his last. It was getting to be too risky.

Any ill-feelings I had towards the commodore were now a thing of the past. I wished him well and hope he was rated a rear-admiral before he retired. (After all, I had learnt later that when he'd appeared at the pool that day he'd been very drunk.)

The next catastrophe concerning Nuisance was again at the pool. I'd been given two days leave and decided to laze round the base all day and go into Cape Town at night. Joyce had been transferred to Durban. Nuisance had not been seen on the aerodrome for about 10 days, but the LAM informed me that he was knocking about round Simon's Town.

On the second day of my leave, about two o'clock in the afternoon, I had just done two lengths of the pool, watched by three Wrens who were also off duty, when Nuisance flopped down where I lay. He ignored the girls' calls to join them and I rubbed his drooping ears and tickled his chin. He licked my arm with that great leathery tongue and his tail swept the concrete slabs.

I heard a buzzing sound and, looking up, saw a hovering hornet. Nuisance didn't like any kind of insect and I had seen him rear up many times and catch a fly in his great jaws. Exit one more plague carrier.

Nuisance was now standing up watching the persistent hornet circling his head and, before I could stop him, had leapt up and caught the striped insect in his jaws. He soared into the air, all four feet leaving the ground, with a lion-like roar of pain. Then he spat out the crushed insect. He was whirling in circles and barking continually and I knew he'd been stung. I grabbed him and opened his mouth. There was a red spot in the middle of his tongue, which was swelling rapidly.

I jumped up and ran in the direction of the sick-bay, Nuisance following but stopping every few yards to rub his tongue against one of his front legs. I dashed in, ignoring the male nurse who sat at the reception desk, and made for the SMO's room down the corridor.

I opened the door and the surgeon, who had been writing on a card, looked up and asked:

"What's the matter, seen a ghost?"

"No sir, it's Nuisance. He's just been stung on the tongue by a hornet." The surgeon jumped to his feet as Nuisance came in the door. His eyes were watering and I could see that he was in pain.

The doctor told me to hold the dog still and I did so while he examined Nuisance's mouth, then he asked.

"How long since he was bitten?"

"Not more than two or three minutes, sir, why is it serious?"

"Any sting in the mouth to a man or animal can be serious, even fatal. Depends on how soon medical assistance is obtained. The trouble is that the swelling can close the breathing passages in the throat, then we have to do a tracheotomy — that is, put a tube inside a slit made in the lower part of the throat so the patient can breathe while we reduce the swelling.'

I felt panic spread through me and asked:

132

"Is that what you've got to do to Nuisance?"

"We'll know in the next few minutes. I've got serum here that will help check the swelling. I'm going to inject it into Nuisance's tongue right next to the sting. Now I'm going to give you a roll of bandage. I want you to place it under Nuisance's tongue and let it rest on his lower teeth, then hold his tongue while I give him this injection. We'd better have a couple of my attendants in to hold his body still, you'll have plenty to worry about holding his tongue. It'll be pretty painful for a few seconds, and I know how strong the dog is."

He called down the corridor for two assistants and they pinned Nuisance with difficulty on the surgery table while I held the bandage and the tongue. When the commander injected I had to hold his head with all my strength, and I kept whispering in his ear trying to calm him. Then the surgeon had finished and allowed Nuisance to sit up.

The Great Dane's mouth kept opening and closing, the commander dismissed his two aides and turned to me, saying.

"Give him five minutes and I'll examine him again, the anti-toxin should be doing its job by that time, reducing the swelling, I mean. If not, there's no other course but to put that tube in his throat."

I sat trembling on a chair in the surgery and the commander mixed me a drink of some sorts, made me gulp it down and told me it would help me to relax. Five minutes later, as Nuisance sat on the table making small whimpering noises, the MO asked me to open his mouth again. Using a small pencil-like torch, he examined Nuisance's tongue, switched off the electric bulb, stood up and smiled.

"Caught it in time. The swelling has already gone down and, with his constitution, his own body's curative powers are taking over now. But I'm taking no chances. We'll keep him here all night in case of a relapse, but that's unlikely now.

"He can't have any lager, but we must see he has plenty of liquid for the next 24 hours, what will he drink?"

"Milk sir, but he'll drink it only if there's nothing else available." I saw Nuisance tucked up in a hospital bed and he was already looking a bit more perky. A sick-bay attendant had a bottle of milk in his hand and was trying to make Nuisance drink from a rubber tube attached to the bottle neck.

I took it from him and placed it in Nuisance's mouth. He looked at me as he tasted it. A look that was both accusing and questioning.

I stared into his eyes and said:

"Come on Nuisance, drink this — then big eats and lager tomorrow. Rum too."

His floppy ears rose at the sound of these words and he probably thought I meant this was to be his next drink when he'd finished off the milk. By this time he'd also learnt what the word rum meant, so he guzzled down the milk.

I stroked his head and he yawned, licked my wrist then laid his head

133

on the pillow for a kip. Five minutes later he was snoring soundly.

Later that night I saw the MO and asked how Nuisance was progressing.

"Swelling's about gone altogether, call for him about nine in the morning and I'll sign his release."

"What about special kinds of food or drink for the next few days, sir?"

"Not required, no limits, he can even have plenty of lager — he's good as new."

"Thanks very much, sir. I think he'd have died without your help."

"Oh I don't know, plenty of animals have recovered from hornet stings without medical help."

"But they've a better chance with it sir, haven't they?"

"That's one prognosis I can't argue with."

Next morning just after nine I fetched Nuisance from hospital and there was no sign that he'd been ill. I took him along to the ratings' dining hall, explained what had happened to the chief cook who grinned and opened the galley door as Nuisance bounded in, big black nose sniffing at the aroma of cooking meat.

A Sailor's Farewell

In October 1943 I went into the sick-bay at Wingfield where the SMO was waiting to give me a routine injection for anti-tetanus. Everyone in the Royal Navy received preventive booster shots whenever our medical records showed they were due. It worked out at an average of one every two months.

As I put on my coat again after receiving the injection the SMO asked me to sit down in his private office and took a large photo album from a bookshelf and said,

"Here's something that will interest you. Photographs of Nuisance taken from 1941 onwards with notes I've made at the side or underneath. I've been on this base since January 1941, and due to be transferred home any day now. How much do you know about Nuisance's early life?"

I explained about meeting Benjamin Chaney and related some of the comical incidents he'd told me about Nuisance before entering the Royal Navy. The surgeon rocked with laughter as I told him about the affair of the ripped pillow and then I told him,

"I didn't know you were that interested in Nuisance sir, keeping notes of him and records of his service."

"Tell you a secret. I'm damned jealous of your relationship with that dog; don't know how you managed it. Still, that's your affair, but count yourself lucky. God knows I've tried ever since he started coming here. But one thing I will tell you – I like that dog just as much as you do."

I told the doctor about the surgeon-commander at Simon's Town who'd cured Nuisance's limp and how the dog rushed up to shake his hand whenever they met. The commander smiled ruefully and said he wished it was himself who'd performed that simple little operation.

He opened the album and the first photograph showed Nuisance lying on a train seat and the date 1940 written alongside. The second was of the dog sleeping in a bed at the Union Jack Club in Cape Town.

Some of these photographs are illustrated in the book, so I will not go into laboured descriptions, but it is necessary to describe the details, as I have not yet referred to them, and they are all important aspects or highlights of Nuisance's life.

A postcard-type photograph showed Nuisance being held on to by a rating dressed in fore-and-aft rig, with a smaller Great Dane attached to a leash gripped by a rating in square rig. The smaller dog had a spray of flowers fixed by some means to the top of its head. The occasion, and who the dogs were, was explained by an inset on the right hand side of the postcard – Nuisance's marriage to the Great Dane Adinda, at Hout .

135

Bay in June 1941. But I asked the surgeon-commander if he knew the details and aftermath of this event and he smiled,

"Well not all of them, but I can fill you in on a lot."

He started his reminiscences.

Apparently a woman who lived in Ermelo, about 1000 miles up country from Cape Town, had a Great Dane bitch named Adinda whose pedigree was impeccable. The owner wanted Adinda to have a litter of puppies, but there was no suitable prospective sire in or around Ermelo. So she and the bitch travelled to the home of a friend who lived near Cape Town in the hope of finding a bachelor Great Dane to father Adinda's family.

Hearing of this dilemma, a local businessman decided he would fetch Nuisance from Simon's Town to be viewed by Adinda's owner, and see if she approved of the dog. He obtained a copy of Nuisance's pedigree from the SA Kennel Union showing his sire to be Koning, his dam Diana, and Nuisance's own registration Pride of Rondebosch.

This pedigree was a first-class one.

The businessman approached the Admiralty, explained the situation and the CO of *HMS Afrikander I* sent a squad of ratings in search of Nuisance. He was eventually found, granted seven days leave (and full rations for that period) and the businessman-matchmaker took Nuisance in his car

Just Nuisance meets his pups, Victor and Wilhelmina, for the first time on their arrival at Cape Town railway station, from the Transvaal. The pups received a mayoral welcome, and the station and its precincts were thronged for the occasion. The pups, born at Ermelo, were later auctioned for war funds.

from Simon's Town to Adinda and her mistress.

Adinda's owner approved of the canine able seaman and so the 'marriage' was arranged. Where the honeymoon was spent is not recorded, but when Adinda returned to Ermelo it was plain that she would in a few months time be giving birth to a family.

On August 7, 1941 Adinda produced two young puppies, one male and the other a female. It was decided that when they were old enough they would be taken to Cape Town to meet their famous sire and be auctioned off to the highest bidders. The money would be donated to the war effort. There would also be an official public reception held for Nuisance and his two offspring which would be attended by the leading dignitaries of Cape Town.

On October 25, 1941 the puppies, who had been named Victor and Wilhelmina, arrived at Cape Town station to a tumultuous welcome.

Nuisance, who had been brought from Simon's Town to be honoured along with his pups, arrived in a lorry bedecked by a Union Jack. He was sitting in the back, licking wounds he'd received in a melee with a bunch of other dogs. A naval rating had been detailed as his escort, to restrain him from running away because the canine able seaman hated pomp and ceremony.

However, Victor, Wilhelmina and Nuisance were officially welcomed by the Mayor and Mayoress of Cape Town at the station entrance and many other important personages were present. Police, Boy Scouts, Pressmen and, of course, crowds of his oppos were gathered in a large turnout round the station. A couple of times Nuisance attempted to break away from all this fuss, although one puppy sat gazing at his sire with admiration and the other had tried to reach his father's side. Nuisance ignored them for a few minutes, but then condescended to walk over and lick their faces. At which they bounded about, claiming more indications of affection from dad – but he'd done his bit for the day and his great head nudged them away.

Carpets had been laid out for the canine feet to walk on, flags and streamers were tied across the length and breadth of Adderley Street and a motorcade, composed of the Mayor's official limousine and cars carrying other notable persons, was led by a car containing Nuisance and his pups.

Cheering crowds lined both pavements and the dogs were taken to the City Hall where the pups were to be auctioned. The auction raised hundreds of pounds. Jack Stubbs bought the female pup while Lady Robinson bought Victor, all proceeds going to war funds.

I sat spellbound as the surgeon showed me the collection of photographs and asked him if he had any spare negatives of them. He shook his head, saying he'd obtained them from Pressmen or from the *Cape Times* and *Cape Argus* newspaper files. He suggested that I do the same but, to my regret, I never attempted to do this. He explained that the businessman who'd arranged the marriage of Nuisance was a personal acquaintance of his.

He was a kindly man, that surgeon, besides being a great admirer of Nuisance, and I was deeply grateful to him for supplying me with details of what I regarded as an important part of Nuisance's life from a domestic viewpoint.

Till then I'd had no idea that Nuisance had a son and daughter, as dependants.

I didn't see Nuisance at the air station for a couple of weeks, but our LAM said he'd been seen knocking about round Cape Town docks. Many of the ships anchored in the docks received visits from Nuisance and there were stories of how some of their crews (both Royal and Merchant navies) had tried to keep him aboard, but never succeeded. He always managed to disembark just before they sailed. I think the crafty canine AB raised his ears as the ships started their engines, or he saw the mooring ropes being cast off. He had no fancy for a long sea voyage as an extra AB, so invariably he bounded ashore.

In November I was sitting in my quarters when there was a knock on the door. An officer's steward stood there and told me I was to report to the CO straight away.

Wondering what I had done wrong, as I'd never received such a summons to attend my commanding officer before, I donned my coat, put my uniform in order and went along to the CO's office.

Tucking my cap under my arm, I walked in and stood at attention before his desk. He was reading a signal sheet.

With relief I noted he was smiling, so it couldn't be anything serious.

I was wrong; it was serious.

"Stand easy Sisson. I've sent for you to do me a great favour, if you will. I am not making it an order, that would be neither fair nor ethical, as it does not come within the scope of your official duties. Regard it as an urgent request for you to help me out of a difficult situation."

I had no hesitation in my reply as this man was the finest naval officer I'd ever known.

"Certainly sir, I'd consider it an honour."

"It's Nuisance. I know that dog regards you with the greatest affection. Are you aware that a cruiser, *HMS Redoubt*, is anchored here at the Cape?"

"No sir, I didn't know that."

"Well she is – and Nuisance has killed their mascot. A dog. I'm not aware of the full details; her Captain is forwarding a report to me. Evidently, and quite naturally, the crew is incensed and have threatened to harm Nuisance who is being held for his own safety in the dockyard's senior naval officer's quarters.

"I've spoken to Commander Shakespear at *Afrikander* by telephone and we both agree it would be much better if Nuisance was brought here rather than to Simon's Town till the ship sails – or a few days have passed and things have quietened down. I have a chit here authorising our motor transport section to provide you with a jeep so you can fetch him. Will you do that?"

"Of course I will, sir. But, with respect, if Nuisance killed a dog it must have attacked or threatened him. He's been in my company dozens of times when other dogs have been near and, unless they run towards him, he ignores them."

"I know that and I've no doubt that when I receive the report from *Redoubt's* captain that's what will have been the cause. I suggest you make all speed young man."

"Aye, aye sir."

I hurried out of the door, collected the jeep and set off for the dockyard.

When I arrived a petty officer led me to the Senior Naval Officer's quarters and I entered and gave the SNO an envelope handed to me by Captain Farquhar. Nuisance was tied up with a piece of stout rope round his neck, the other end fastened to the leg of a table. I approached him and he reared up on his hind legs, placed his paws on each of my shoulders and licked my face.

Other than a nasty gash on his right front leg, he seemed unharmed. The SNO said,

"Get him out of here. I've already had *Redoubt's* captain and first lieutenant in here vowing retribution on Nuisance. Give Captain Farquhar my compliments and ask him to keep the dog away for a few days, at least."

I untied Nuisance and he trotted happily by my side and hopped into the passenger seat of the jeep. I never knew whether it was pure laziness or enjoyment, but Nuisance would always show excitement when riding in anything on wheels. He'd even jump on the hand-pulled bomb trolley, after it had been detached from the jeep that pulled it, for a 20-yard trip to the aircraft where the bombs were loaded underneath the wings.

Anyway, I drove back to Wingfield and called at the sick-bay first so the SMO could dress the gash on Nuisance's leg.

The commander washed it carefully in disinfectant, put some kind of ointment over the wound murmuring, as he put a pad on it and taped it securely, "Not deep enough to be stitched. Bring him in tomorrow and I'll check for sepsis. How did he come by this?"

I explained about *Redoubt's* mascot and he whistled, then remarked,

"What kind of dog was it that he killed? I guarantee it must have been a large hound; he wouldn't have killed a small one. Plays with them, you know that, and it must have attacked him first. Nuisance isn't a vicious dog."

"Exactly what I told the CO sir," I replied.

I took Nuisance over to the CO's office, told him what the SNO had said and, to my surprise, Captain Farquhar held out his hand and said as he gave me a firm handshake,

"I'm much obliged to you Sisson. I have a great respect for Nuisance myself, though I don't suppose it shows in my manner towards him."

"We all know that sir, officers and ratings here at Wingfield; with respect, however, your seeming impartiality isn't very successful."

"I'll be damned, I thought no one knew. Now, as to Nuisance, can you arrange for him to stay at Wingfield for a few days?" He grinned and added,

"The leading air mechanic will fix him up with a bed and all his meals sir, but there's the question of him sneaking out past the guardroom and slipping ashore."

Captain Farquhar replied: "I'll look after that problem. The guardroom staff will be warned that Nuisance is barred from shore leave for the next seven days – though, of course, that will not be on his conduct sheet. Let's say he's in protective custody. Alright Sisson, dismissed and thank you once again."

"Seeing it was necessary to protect Nuisance sir, it was a pleasure."

A few days later a memo appeared on all the notice boards at Wingfield. It stated that, after an inquiry by senior naval officers into the death of *HMS Redoubt's* mascot, it had been established that Able Seaman Just Nuisance was only defending himself against attack by another canine. He was exonerated of all blame.

I could have cheered when I first read it. Come to think of it, I did.

The wound on Nuisance's leg was now healed completely, and as *HMS Redoubt* had left port I took Nuisance into Cape Town that night.

The manager at the Texas Bar had already been inaugurated into Nuisance's new favourite tipple of lager-and-rum and, though I don't know how, had managed to obtain a few bottles of navy issue rum, some for me and others for Nuisance.

We went up to the balcony, and had become such regular patrons that anyone passing me on the stairs carrying the chamber pot of lager-and-rum seldom giggled or laughed.

Nuisance, as usual, dissected his meat pies and wolfed down the meat, then waited for his pot to be re-filled. When he'd lapped up the second potful no longer would he walk away, but licked all round the inside of the container until rinsing it out was a needless exercise. Not a drop was left, either at the bottom or round the sides.

We caught the last train back to Wingfield from town, having spent an uneventful but pleasant night at the City Hall. For once Nuisance had been satisfied at most of the acts and appeared to sleep when he didn't like some of the others.

I pointed him in the direction of the billets and he held out his paw for a good-night handshake and rasped his tongue across the back of my fingers as I took his paw, then shot off into the night.

Next day I slept late, and in the afternoon went to the pool.

The LAM was there and told me he'd been granted a "make and mend" (the whole day free from duty) as he'd worked on an engine till two in the morning. He also said that Nuisance, when on the aerodrome, came into the hangar where the aircraft was parked every day, wandering round the undercarriage and licking the fuselage.

Then he'd race around it three or four times and trot away.

Nuisance appeared alongside the pool, took a running dive, all four legs outspread, and flopped right on top of a Wren who was swimming by. Luckily she was a powerful swimmer and attractive, too. But when she re-surfaced from under the canine monster her language should have shrivelled the dog's coat.

He glanced at her disdainfully, as if she'd no business being in the pool with a champion swimmer such as he was, then dog-paddled his way to the far end, spat out a jet of water from his jaws and paddled back, and one of his oppos helped him out.

After bathing for an hour or so, I had a quiet word with the LAM about getting a drink at the NAAFI. He nodded and we started walking the 300 yards or so to the canteen.

Nuisance, curious as always, followed us then trotted ahead in the lead.

I called out to him, "Lager and big eats Nuisance."

He was walking slightly off course of the refreshment building but, on hearing my words, his nose (as if it was a compass needle) swung directly in line for the source of lager.

Suddenly, as we walked across the sandy soil dotted with the odd tufts of parched grass, Nuisance stopped, held one paw off the ground and barked. He started running in circles around one particular area and, remembering the scorpion episode, I murmured to the LAM.

"He's found a scorpion, I saw him kill one a few months ago. Let's get a bit closer and you'll see how he does it."

I saw it wasn't a scorpion but a snake about 40 cm in length, no thicker at any part of its body than a pencil and it had a vicious, flat little head. It was nearly the same colour as the sand along which it was writhing.

Although in various lectures our SMO had warned us of these snakes, this was the first time I'd seen one. Apparently, like the scorpion, it could inflict a nasty bite but was rarely fatal if medical treatment was obtained quickly. I'd expected a cobra to be marked with bright colours on its body, but this one was either too young or had just shed its skin.

It moved remarkably quickly, sliding across the sand twisting first one way then another. But Nuisance darted ahead and, turning his hind quarters towards it, those tremendously strong legs kicked out a pile of sand which covered the snake. A few seconds later the reptile's head emerged from the mound and it wriggled away once more. Nuisance ran ahead and repeated the process. We walked nearer, but Nuisance got himself between us and the snake, nudging our legs with his body as if to say:

"That's near enough; leave this to me."

We could now hear the soft hissing the snake was making and its minute forked tongue was darting in and out of the small mouth. We also thought we could glimpse the twin fangs through which it injected its poison when biting.

There was a low rumbling from Nuisance's half-open mouth, and once again he kicked sand over the snake, repeating this action at least a dozen times. The snake by this time was in a frenzy of anger. The hissing grew louder and, instead of moving forward as before, began to turn in very small circles. I realised the sense behind Nuisance's method of attack. He wanted the snake to grow bewildered as the creature found every move it made was blocked by the dog, and it now maintained a position in a very restricted area.

Nuisance kicked a bigger heap of sand over the snake than before, a mound about 20 cm in height, then advanced, put one front paw on top of the mound, lifted up his other paw – and waited . . .

The snake's head appeared from the bottom of the pile and, before it could wriggle more of its body free, Nuisance's uplifted paw came down on the flat head with lightning speed – stamping into the sandy soil and twisting as if grinding husks of corn.

He stepped back, waited about 30 seconds, then using his right paw scraped some of the sand away, exposing the body of the snake. The flat head, from the tip of the jaw to a point on its body 50 mm back, was half the thickness it had been before, a pulped mass of flesh. But although obviously dead or dying, Nuisance wasn't satisfied. He turned his hind-quarters towards it and let fly with both rear legs just as he had done with the scorpion, and watched as it flew in the air and bounded away to where it had dropped.

We followed and found him pawing away at the snake which still twisted about but, in two places, the body was nearly severed. Nuisance reared up on his hind legs and brought both his front paws down on the broken body, squashing it even flatter. The snake, except for an occasional twitch, was now still.

I patted Nuisance's head and he trotted up and down, tail sweeping in wide arcs. Then he stood with one foot off the ground, pug nose stuck in the air – reminding me of an ancient gladiator who had just vanquished an opponent.

I took out my handkerchief and wrapped the snake's body in it, being careful to hold it by the tail – it was possible that some venom remained in the crushed head. I wanted the SMO to see this dead reptile; he'd been a little dubious when I'd told him about the scorpion.

Nuisance was looking at the LAM and I in bewilderment as we headed for the sick-bay instead of the canteen.

We entered the swing doors and I nodded at the male nurse at his desk, and walked down the corridor to the SMO's room. I knocked and entered, Nuisance following me inside, while the LAM waited by the door.

The surgeon was reading a medical journal but, on seeing Nuisance, he stood up and stroked the dog's head, turned to me and asked:

"Not another hornet sting Sisson?"

"No sir. Nuisance is fine. I've brought you a small trophy he's just killed." I placed the handkerchief containing the snake's body on his desk. He unwrapped the white linen cloth and whistled, saying,

"A cape cobra – and you say Nuisance killed it. How?"

I explained the tactics Nuisance had adopted and he looked at the Great Dane with pleased admiration.

"I'm going to have this stuffed and hung on the wall of my office. If it was anyone else who'd told me this, I'd have said it was a tall story."

"Not this time, sir, there's my LAM outside. He saw the whole thing too."

We then went to the back door of the canteen where I treated all three of us to a quart of lager, and the manageress found a lump of mutton for Nuisance. To my amazement, he ate only half the meat and hardly touched the lager, and an apprehensive thought entered my head. What if some of the venom had somehow got into Nuisance's bloodstream; this would account for his loss of appetite.

The LAM went back to his billet after finishing his drink as I wanted to visit the sick-bay again. I took Nuisance along with me and was lucky to catch the SMO just before he left for his lunch.

Explaining my fears, the SMO shook his head and said the chances of Nuisance having any venom in him were nil. There'd have been a very noticeable swelling on his body, which there wasn't, and he'd have probably been having mild convulsions by this time.

Then he said, "For the last week the chief cook at the ratings' dining hall has informed me that the dog's lost his appetite. In fact I was going to ask you to bring him round to the surgery here this afternoon, but I'll give him a check-up now that he's here.

"It could be a slight attack of worms, but a worm-cake would clear that up in a couple of days. However, he doesn't show any signs of having that. Would you wait outside, Sisson – some of the tests I'll do are a bit gruesome to the layman?

I sat outside the doctor's surgery for more than an hour – then he called me inside, motioned me to sit down and said,

"There's good news and bad news. First there's nothing seriously wrong with any of his vital organs, but his nervous reflexes are not what they should be, also his pulse and blood pressure are abnormally high, I won't go into medical terms; you'd not understand them, anyway.

"What it boils down to is that, in spite of his strong appearance, he's suffering from physical and nervous exhaustion – been doing too much each day for too many months. What he requires is a good long rest, and I don't mean here in the sick-bay. Remember I'm not a vet, and that's what he needs – someone who specialises in animal diseases – and confinement to open-air kennels where he can get proper treatment, fresh air and not exhaust himself by running around on the loose.

"As it happens I know just the chap, he's a miracle worker when it comes to curing sick animals. I'll give him a ring on the telephone, but till he fetches Nuisance I'm going to keep him in the sick-bay. Don't worry, this chap will soon have him fit again."

To be truthful I had noticed a certain lack of vigour in Nuisance during the past few months but thought it was just a passing phase which would clear up on its own. After all, he'd not been actually ill, and this was the first I'd heard about his loss of appetite for a week or more.

Nuisance had been sitting in a corner glancing from the doctor to me as if he understood what had been said. Then the commander asked if I would help to settle Nuisance into a hospital bed in a small private ward. This I did, but he looked at me reproachfully, as I left him lying in bed and shook his paw before going back to my quarters.

I was pleased there was nothing seriously wrong with Nuisance, but worried nevertheless. I recalled the SMO's words about the vet and felt less depressed. The surgeon was a straightforward chap who told all his patients what was wrong with them, serious or not. If Nuisance had been really ill he would never have put on a bedside manner, like so many doctors did, and would have bluntly explained what was the trouble – and if it could be cured.

Next day, the last week in November 1943, Nuisance was taken to the kennels belonging to Fred Burrington, at Wetton, near Cape Town.

The SMO, myself and several other ratings stood near the sick-bay steps at Wingfield and waved goodbye to him as the vehicle started on its journey to Wetton. Burrington, although the Royal Navy had offered to pay all expenses for Nuisance's stay at the kennels, refused to accept a penny. He too was fond of Nuisance and I knew the dog would get the best treatment available.

His confinement in the kennels was reported in both of Cape Town's newspapers and Burrington was inundated with daily phone calls from citizens of the Peninsula enquiring about Nuisance's response to treatment.

He was discharged from the kennels on January 1 1944, but Burrington advised all naval bases round the Peninsula that, although Nuisance was now fit and well again, a careful watch should be kept on his diet and what he was given to drink.

The dog, after discharge from the kennels, was at Simon's Town for a few weeks and I asked the SMO if my supplying him with rum-and-lager had contributed to his illness. He shook his head.

"No Sisson. If anything, it could well have kept him on his feet for a little longer before he became ill. His trouble was too much exertion spread over a long period. The reason Mr Burrington had put out this warning about Nuisance's diet, is not to do with what he ate and drank before going to the kennels, but a normal precaution the same as human beings are given after being ill – the sort of things that he ought to eat and drink that will help to build up his strength again."

I was very relieved at the surgeon's words. The thought that my tots of rum might have been responsible for his condition had haunted me for several days.

On February 7, 1944 the CO sent for me and informed me that he'd received a signal from the Admiralty ordering me back to the UK. I was to leave in three days' time. He shook hands, told me he would be sorry

144

to lose me, and wished me all good luck. He added that, as from that moment, I was on leave till it was time to board the troopship at Cape Town docks.

I asked him if I could borrow a jeep from the transport section that afternoon as I would like to see Nuisance and take him for a run in the vehicle before bidding him goodbye.

I was ashamed of the moisture in my eyes as I made this request, but this fine commanding officer reached across his desk, grasped my shoulder and, as if speaking to his own son, said:

"I know how you feel Sisson. Over my years in the service I've had to say goodbye to shipmates who have been like brothers to me. The only way to avoid a good deal of grief is to give thanks that at least you had the pleasure of their company for a time."

He reached out, scribbled a message on a form and handed it to me. Through misty eyes I saw that he had allocated me a jeep for three full days. I managed to stammer out my thanks, but he smiled and said it was the least he could do.

After we left the CO's office I picked up my jeep from the MT section and drove straight to Simon's Town. After asking where Nuisance might be, I finally located him on the steps of the United Services Institute. As soon as he saw me, Nuisance ran down and put both paws on my shoulders and licked my cheeks, no doubt tasting the salt of my tears on them. He looked a lot thinner than when I'd last seen him, but seemed to be in good health.

I led him to the jeep and his tail wagged with excitement. With his old zest he jumped into the passenger seat, holding his pug nose high as we passed out of the base's entrance. I drove him for many miles round the coast and stopped several times to give him a run. Then I returned to *Afrikander* at Simon's Town and left him at the same spot I'd picked him up, hugging his neck and shaking his paw before I left.

I did the same thing the next day. But as this was the last occasion I had in which to say goodbye, I dropped him off at the United Services Institute and, as I clasped him round the neck, I was sobbing like a child. He seemed to understand that this was to be our final sight of each other, because he repeatedly licked my face clean of tears and placed one paw on my arm like a parent consoling a child.

I ran to the jeep, leapt into the seat and drove off without looking back.

On February 10, 1944 I stood at the stern of a troopship, looking back at the looming mass of Table Mountain, and beyond towards Simon's Town, and hoped Nuisance was having big eats and lager, if he was allowed it.

More than a fortnight later we docked at Gourock in Scotland and I was sent on 16 days leave at home. On arriving there I was greeted by my parents and a smaller version of Nuisance, called King. I had written of Nuisance to my father and several times while on leave and, if I happened to be day-dreaming and King was near me, I'd call out,

"Come on Nuisance".

In May 1944, while I was stationed at Lee-on-Solent near Portsmouth, I received an airmail letter informing me that Nuisance had died and been buried near Simon's Town. I was dismal company for several weeks, till I recalled the parting words of Captain Farquhar at Wingfield:

"At least you had the pleasure of his company for a time."

Whenever I think of Nuisance – which is often, even after 40 years or more have passed – those few words are a source of consolation.

———————————————

GREAT DANE
JUST NUISANCE,
ABLE SEAMAN R.N.
H.M.S. AFRIKANDER,
1940 - 44.
DIED 1 APRIL 1944,
AGE 7 YEARS.

One of Just Nuisance's descendants, at his famous forebear's grave at Klaver Camp above Simon's Town. Wrapped in a White Ensign, Nuisance was buried there with naval honours in April 1944.

Epilogue

There are many accounts, myths, and rumours surrounding the death of Able Seaman Just Nuisance (b. 1/4/37, d. 1/4/44) and his period of service with the Royal Navy, August 25, 1939 to April 1, 1944. After a great deal of research the truth is as follows.

In late November 1943, because of poor health, Nuisance was admitted for treatment to the Home Kennels owned by Fred Burrington, of Wetton, near Cape Town. He was discharged as 'fit and well' on January 1, 1944. He escaped from Simon's Town Naval Base in January 1944, and was twice observed to jump off moving buses and lorries after this escape. He injured his back legs on both occasions.

On March 6, 1944 he was re-admitted to the Burrington kennels for examination and treatment. Mr Burrington states:

"Nuisance knew he was going to die; he often looked at me appealingly for the help which no one could give him. One of his rear legs was shrivelling and soon the other one was affected. I asked for professional advice from veterinary surgeons, but all agreed the case was hopeless.

"I told the naval authorities he would have to be destroyed, and they asked me to put him to sleep. I did not have the courage or inclination for this task."

He was admitted later in March to the Royal Naval Hospital at Simon's Town, given a bed ticket and medical chart, in exactly the same manner as a human rating patient. In his medical folder are X-ray and medical examination reports, signed by surgeon-lieutenants, surgeon-lieutenant-commanders, and one by the Senior Medical Officer, Captain H.E.Y. White.

His illness was diagnosed as "Paralysis of the sciatic nerve".

There are records of his temperature, pulse rate and respiration rate. He became so ill that finally he had to be put to sleep. Ironically and tragically, this was done on his birthday, April 1, 1944, aged seven years.

At 11.30 a.m. on Saturday April 2, 1944 he was buried with full naval honours at Klaver Camp near Simon's Town. Nuisance's body was wrapped in a Royal Navy White Ensign and as he was lowered into the grave, buglers sounded the Last Post and a party fired a volley over the grave. The funeral party was commanded by Lieutenant-Commander V. W. Pearce RN and more than 100 officers and ratings filed past the grave.

The majority of the mourners had tears in their eyes.

During the writing of this book I have received letters, photographs, newspaper clippings, all dealing with Nuisance from ex-naval officers and

COPY

BED TICKET ROYAL HOSPITAL AT _Cape Hospital_ WARD 2.

Serial Number	o o o.
Surname of Patient	N U I S A N C E.
Christian Names of Patient	Just.
Rank or Rating	A·B. S·A·N·F (V).
Age	7 years Date of Birth 1st April 1936.
Official Number	1
Number on Ship's Books	1
Port Division	South Africa.
Religion	Canine Divinity League. (anti Vivisectionist)
Ship or Establishment	H·M·S. "AFRIKANDER"
Disease or Injury. 1. Reasons for {	(eg. motor accident) N·O·D. Paralisis of Sciatic Nerve.
2. Destroyed	Poor General Condition
Date and Time of Admission	0900. 2nd March 1944.
Date and Time of Discharge	a.m. 7th March 1944.
Disposal	Transfered to Welton Vetinary Hospital
Date of Survey if Invalided	Discharged Dead -1/4/44
Name, Address and Relationship of Nearest Relative	Wife Judy. Prince alfred Hotel Simonstown. S.A.
Previous Occupation	Bone Crusher.

Sta. 95/29.

Just Nuisance's last hospital bed-ticket, recording his death on April 1, 1944.

ratings who knew him personally. The same applies to citizens of the RSA, ~om the Cape Peninsula, Johannesburg, Durban, Port Elizabeth, East London, and many other towns and cities of the Republic. They forwarded photographs and articles about this beloved animal. In all I received 468 letters that would help me complete this manuscript, most of them asking where they could obtain a copy of the book.

One letter brought to me feelings of nostalgic grief.

It was from an ex-chief petty officer who I will not name because it may cause him embarrassment. He was a leading seaman at the time of Nuisance's funeral, and had been awarded the Distinguished Service Medal by HM King George VI, at Buckingham Palace in 1940, for gallantry against the enemy at Narvik, in Norway, while serving aboard a British destroyer.

He confessed to me in his letter that, as he filed past Nuisance's grave, in his hand he held a length of his medal ribbon, which he dropped into the grave. "In my opinion it was no more than Able Seaman Nuisance deserved, not for gallantry against the enemy but for the comradeship, loyalty, assistance, and great affection he had for his oppos."

There are rumours that Nuisance's body will be disinterred and reburied in a grave that is not as remote as that in which he now lies. I hope this does not happen – let an old sailor rest in peace.

Below I submit an epitaph in poetic form which I am sure Nuisance would consider suitable. The poem is my own.

MY LAST VOYAGE
For if I die in battle, or of disease at sea,
Wrap me in a hammock, let the oceans cover me.
But if by the hand of fate I breathe my last ashore,
Bury me in earth a fathom deep, and disturb my rest no more.

Sleep on Nuisance, and may your last voyage be one of calm seas and fair winds; there'll never be another like you; the mould was broken when you were formed.

You are remembered with affection by a whole generation in your homeland and will be for many years to come, wherever oppos gather.
T. D. Sisson